# PERSPECTIVES ON LATIN AMERICA

# PERSPECTIVES ON LATIN AMERICA

Edited by Samuel L. Baily

and Ronald T. Hyman

MACMILLAN PUBLISHING CO., INC.
*New York*

COLLIER MACMILLAN PUBLISHERS
*London*

Macmillan Publishing Co., Inc.
866 Third Avenue, New York, N. Y. 10022
Collier-Macmillan Canada Ltd.

---

Library of Congress Cataloging in Publication Data

Baily, Samuel L
  Perspectives on Latin America.

  (Latin America series)
  1. Latin America—Addresses, essays, lectures.
I. Hyman, Ronald T., joint author.  II. Title.
F1406.7.B34           918'.03'308           73-10689
ISBN 0-02-505830-4

---

First Printing 1974

Printed in the United States of America

*We dedicate this book to
the forty-five members of the NDEA Institute
of Latin American History held on the
campus of Rutgers University in the
summer of 1967. It was they
who provided the inspiration for the book.*

# CONTENTS

# PREFACE TO THE SERIES

THIS SERIES OF BOOKS on Latin America grew out of a summer institute we directed at Rutgers University in 1967. The institute was sponsored by Rutgers University and supported financially by the National Defense Education Act (NDEA). We invited forty-five teachers from all over the United States to live on our campus for six weeks, to study Latin American issues, and to design with us ways of teaching these issues to their students. We also brought in leading scholars and journalists with special knowledge of Latin America to help us in our work.

These books reflect what we learned from our institute experience. The task of translating our ideas into a series of books, however, has not been easy. Two general problems have confronted us and it is well to recognize them here since their solutions have become the backbone of all of these books. First, there is the question arising from history and the social sciences: how can a person from one country or one culture adequately understand the issues facing a person from another country or another culture? The major obstacle in the path of the North American student who wishes to understand Latin America is his cultural bias. What he will learn about Latin America depends to a considerable extent upon his point of view, or his frame of reference. People see what their frame of reference prepares them to see, and most North Americans are simply not prepared to see Latin America as Latin Americans do.

A person's cultural bias or frame of reference is determined by many things including nationality, social class, religion, economic class, historical heritage, education, and technological skills. Can we in the United States—members of a highly industrialized, predominantly Protestant, democratic society—understand the people of the developing, Catholic, and for the most part authoritarian societies of Latin America? Can we whose revolution is part of the distant past sympathize with the

Mexicans, Bolivians, and Cubans whose revolutions are part of the present? Is it possible for middle class, North American students to understand the life of the inhabitants of the shanty towns surrounding modern cities like Buenos Aires, Rio de Janeiro, Lima, and Santiago? Can we see the world as a variety of Latin Americans see it?

There is no simple answer to these questions. Though we may never be able to remove our own particular cultural bias, we can and must adjust our frame of reference so that we will be able to understand Latin Americans and the issues facing them. If we recognize that we have a cultural bias which determines what we see and we compare our bias with that of the people we are studying, we will have a good chance of understanding what others think and feel.

The second question concerns education: how can we meaningfully teach a person something about the issues facing people in another country? Here again there is no simple answer. We do know, however, that a person will read—and understand what he reads—when the topic is of interest to him and related to his own experience. Furthermore, we believe a reader prefers to examine those topics which call upon him to participate in the search for answers. He is not satisfied with simple, pat answers, for he knows from his own experience that life is complex. Important issues are interrelated and cut across geographical areas and academic disciplines. A person is willing to participate in the search for answers, even though this approach requires a great expenditure of mental and physical effort, because this approach is meaningful and rewarding to him.

We are convinced that people will understand more about Latin America by analyzing a few key issues in depth than by attempting to learn the names of kings, viceroys, military heroes, presidents, capital cities, mountain ranges, rivers, and so forth that so often fill the pages of textbooks. We are also convinced that readers prefer—and will benefit significantly from—the study of the conflict and tension of man's affairs since these things are an important part of reality.

In summary, the books in this series will:

1. Focus on important issues rather than on a chronological coverage of Latin America.

2. Relate Latin American issues to similar issues in the United States.

3. Emphasize differing points of view to help the reader clarify his own frame of reference.

4. Emphasize controversy as a meaningful approach to the teaching of social studies.

5. Permit and encourage the reader to work with the "stuff" of Latin American studies by presenting relevant documents, maps, charts, and photographs.

6. Focus on the questions of when and how we can legitimately formulate generalizations about Latin America, whether or not we can speak of Latin America as a whole, and whether it is the similarities or the differences among the Latin American countries that are more important.

7. Discuss issues which are representative of those facing other sections of the world besides the Western Hemisphere.

The intent of the editors and authors is to present Latin America to the reader in an open-ended way. We recognize that these books can not encompass all of the important information and interpretations about the area. Our purpose is to provide a basis from which the reader can further his understanding of Latin America today.

—*Samuel L. Baily*
*Ronald T. Hyman*
NEW BRUNSWICK, NEW JERSEY
September, 1973

# INTRODUCTION

THIS BOOK, and the series of books of which it is the introductory volume, focuses on Latin America, yet today most North Americans (that is, citizens of the United States) know next to nothing about Latin America and generally take its existence for granted. Few of us know, for example, that Buenos Aires and São Paulo are cities of seven million people; that the Bolivian Congress deliberates in Aymará and Quechua (local Indian languages) as well as in Spanish; that the population of Argentina is predominantly of white European origin; that there are already over 200 million people living in Latin America today; or that Latin America has the fastest growing population of any area of the world.

Not only are we ignorant about Latin America, but our government tends to ignore it. At present our government is most interested in Europe and Asia. The Castro revolution temporarily focused our attention on Latin America and contributed to the development of the Alliance for Progress, but the United States has never given Latin America the kind of aid it gave Europe under the Marshall Plan, or to Japan under the post-World War II occupation, or that it gives to some of the Southeast Asian countries today.

Given our ignorance of Latin America and our government's primary interest in Europe and Asia, is there any reason to study Latin America? We believe that there are a number of important reasons why North Americans should study Latin America, and we wish to make them clear at the outset.

One reason to study Latin America—or any area of the world other than our own—is to understand the issues facing the peoples of this area. We live in a world made up of many different peoples and cultures with which we are having increasing contact. To live in harmony with these peoples, we must understand what they think and feel, what they believe in, and what their aspirations are for themselves and their children.

120    110    100    90    80    70    60    50    40    30
30

20

10
110              100          90

ATLANTIC

OCEAN

Rio Grande
SIERRA MADRE ORIENTAL
SIERRA MADRE OCCIDENTAL

CARIBBEAN SEA

PACIFIC

OCEAN

LLANOS
Rio Orinoco
GUIANA
HIGHLANDS

Equator

COAST MOUNTAINS

Rio    Amazon

SELVAS

ANDES MOUNTAINS

Titicaca

BRAZILIAN
HIGHLANDS

Rio Tombrampro

Rio Paraná

Rio Uruguay

MT.
ACONCAGUA

PAMPA          Rio de la Plata

ATLANTIC

PATAGONIA

OCEAN

Land above
9000 feet

LATIN
AMERICA

0          500          1000
Miles (Approx.)

50          90          80          70          60          50          40          30          20

A second reason to study Latin America which is closely related to the first is that such a study will force us to recognize that we have a cultural bias or a particular frame of reference which determines what we see when we look at the rest of the world. Our cultural bias is determined by such things as our nationality, sex, race, religion, occupation, and class. Thus, for example, a white, Anglo-Saxon, Protestant, North American, male, middle class student will not see or identify with the issues of Latin America in the same way as a black, Catholic, North American, female, lower class waitress or an Indian, Catholic, Bolivian, lower class peasant or a white, Italian, Catholic, Argentine, male, upper class landowner.

The challenge to all of us is to recognize our cultural bias, to understand that it determines in large part what we see, and then to overcome, insofar as possible, the restrictions that this bias places upon our vision. We must attempt to lift ourselves out of our own cultural environment in order to place ourselves inside the cultural environments of the various Latin Americans we are studying. Only in this way will we be able to understand adequately the issues facing a person from another country. Hopefully our study of Latin America will force us to recognize that we have a cultural bias, and to free ourselves from it long enough to understand others as they see themselves.

In addition, there are a number of reasons why North Americans specifically should study Latin America. Latin America is physically close to us and we share a common boundary of more than two thousand miles. Also we have long-standing ties with Latin America. The United States and the Latin American Republics, all former colonies of European powers, gained their political independence at approximately the same time and for similar reasons. They have shared common ideals of freedom and independence, and although these ideals have not been realized in many parts of the Western Hemisphere, the tradition or perhaps the myth of fighting for them remains. The United States also has special ties with Latin America based on the Monroe Doctrine, the Inter-American system, and the Organization of American States.

There are a number of economic reasons why Latin America is important to us. Latin America has been and still is to a considerable degree an important source of raw materials—such as tin, copper, coffee, and bananas—for the United States. Furthermore, Latin America is a significant market for United States manufactured goods such as cars, typewriters, and computers. In addition, there are strategic and political reasons why Latin America is important to us. The Panama Canal and the Caribbean fueling stations were vital to our navy during the early decades of the century, and we went to great lengths to make sure that Germans did not control air strips in Colombia during World War II. Today our government is anxious to keep the Latin American governments friendly to us and to prevent their take-over by Communist regimes. Also, our government finds Latin American support in such international bodies as the United Nations very useful. And finally, Latin America is important to us because a considerable number of our citizens are of Latin American origin: Puerto Ricans both in Puerto Rico and in New York, Chicanos or Mexican Americans in Texas and California, and Cubans in Florida.

All of these reasons add up to an urgent need to study Latin America so that we as citizens of a leading world power situated next to Latin America can function more wisely, humanely, and effectively.


AN OVERVIEW OF THE ESSAYS

The six original essays that follow offer the reader a series of perspectives with which to view Latin America. The first four essays were written by four social scientists: an anthropologist, an historian, an economist, and a political scientist. Each author looks at Latin America through the particular eyes of his field of specialization, and, as he examines Latin America, introduces us to some of the basic concepts of his discipline. The fifth essay, written by a research physicist, examines the rationale and the results of establishing scientific research centers in Latin America. The final essay draws together some of the basic ideas presented in the book and the author suggests how we might most profitably carry on our study of Latin America.

The essays serve three basic functions:

First, they emphasize the fact that different people looking at the same thing will focus on what is important to each one of them. The story of the blind men describing the elephant comes to mind; the man touching the trunk thought the elephant was a tree, the man touching the tail thought it was a rope, and the man touching the side thought it was a wall. No one author tells us, nor can he tell us, "the whole truth." Instead, he sets forth what he knows about Latin America, his viewpoint fashioned by the concepts he uses to describe and interpret the area. For example, Turner uses the concepts of power and influence while Safa uses those of society and subculture.

Second, the essays, and particularly the four social science essays, serve to introduce us to these separate but overlapping fields of study. Street's essay, for example, acquaints us with some of the key concepts of economics such as inflation, monetary policy, and structural economic change. Similarly, Baily emphasizes the historian's reliance on the concepts of the uniqueness of individuals and events, and of historical time perspective.

Third, the essays introduce the reader to Latin America as a challenging and complex topic worthy of study. We see Latin America as a dynamic area with problems of concern to its citizens and to us as its neighbor. Thus, Turner introduces us to the Latin American style of revolution and Safa introduces us to the quality of Latin American society. We see Latin America not simply as a static outpost of Europe or the United States, but as a rapidly growing and constantly changing area. Most importantly, we see Latin Americans facing immense problems and challenges in the 1970s as they attempt to improve the conditions in which they live.

The reader is urged to keep these three functions in mind, because the aim of the authors is to lead him down new paths. Our purpose is not to present a complete picture of Latin America; rather it is to show the reader how to study the area and to tempt him to continue his study by setting forth concepts and information relating to selected topics.

Perhaps the reader will find it helpful to read each essay quickly in order to get a flavor of the book as a whole. Then, he might return to each essay, read it carefully, and compare the various approaches. This should help him understand the edi-

UNITED STATES

ATLANTIC

OCEAN

Rio Grande

Monterrey

MEXICO

Guadalajara

Mexico City

BRITISH HONDURAS

Havana

CUBA

BAHAMA IS.

HAITI

Port-au-Prince

DOMINICAN REPUBLIC

Santo Domingo

PUERTO RICO

JAMAICA

LEEWARD IS.

HONDURAS

Tegucigalpa

CARIBBEAN SEA

WINDWARD IS.

GUATEMALA Guatemala City

EL SALVADOR San Salvador

Managua

NICARAGUA

San José

COSTA RICA

Caracas

TRINIDAD-TOBAGO

VENEZUELA

BRITISH GUIANA

SURINAM

FRENCH GUIANA

PANAMA

Panama City

Medellín

COLOMBIA

Cali

Bogotá

Quito

ECUADOR

Equator

Guayaquil

Río

Amazon

PACIFIC

PERU

Callao

Lima

BRAZIL

Recife

Arequipa

La Paz

Brasilia D.F.

BOLIVIA

Sucre

OCEAN

PARAGUAY

Paraná

Río de Janeiro

Asunción

São Paulo

CHILE

Río

Córdoba

Rosario

URUGUAY

Valparaíso

Santiago

Buenos Aires

Montevideo

Concepción

ARGENTINA

ATLANTIC

OCEAN

Land above 9000 feet

FALKLAND ISLANDS

LATIN AMERICA

⊚ Capital cities

• Important cities

0        500        1000

Miles (Approx.)

TIERRA DEL FUEGO

tors' design and the three functions performed by the essays. But whether the reader uses this strategy or one which suits him better, we hope he will use this book as a springboard for his own future investigations of and decisions about Latin America.

—S.L.B.
R.T.H.

# 1: LATIN AMERICA FROM THE ANTHROPOLOGIST'S VIEWPOINT: COMMUNITY AND CHANGE

## Helen Icken Safa

*Helen Icken Safa, Professor of Urban Planning and
Political Development at Rutgers University, looks at Latin
America through the eyes of an anthropologist. She explains the
traditional and the contemporary culture areas of Latin America,
but her main concern is with the more recent concept of subculture. Unlike the other authors of this book, she focuses on
non-elites and uses the urban proletariat as an example of a
subculture. Her concept of a dual society should be compared with
Street's concept of a dual economy (Chapter 3) and her concept of
continuity should be compared with that of Baily (Chapter 2).
Safa concludes that the challenge in Latin America today is to
incorporate the subordinate subcultures—such as the peasantry and
the urban proletariat—into the mainstream of the Latin American
societies whether by force or by pacific means.*

LATIN AMERICA IS A HETEROGENEOUS AREA. It includes varied races, languages, geographic regions, cultures, religions, and nations. Given such variety, how can we understand this complex area? Is there a pattern which helps us to see it as a coherent whole? Is there a thread linking the different regions and groups of Latin America extending from the past to the present?

The attempt to create an overall framework for looking at Latin America differs from one discipline to another. Anthropologists study the cultures and societies of Latin America. Culture embraces all of the ideas, techniques, values, and behavior patterns which men learn and transmit as part of their particular way of life. Societies, on the other hand, are groups of people who learn and transmit a particular culture. For example, an Indian peasant village in the Mexican highlands may grow maize for sale at a weekly market in exchange for manufactured goods like cloth and farm implements. The Indians of the village are the society, and the food which they produce, where and how they sell their products, and their religious festivals and holidays related to the growing of maize are all elements of their culture.

Each culture is somewhat different because each is the product of different environmental conditions, historical traditions, and stages of technological development. As man's mastery over his environment increased, culture became increasingly complex, and man's dependence on the natural environment lessened. Thus, the pre-Columbian native cultures of South America can be ranked by their stage of technological development, ranging from the primitive hunters and gatherers of the marginal southern plains to the highly complex civilizations of the Andean Inca Empire. The level of technological development in turn largely determines the level of cultural development, and only in the Andean area did agricultural technology produce a surplus large enough to support the permanent, urban, nonagricultural population necessary for a complex civilization. A civilization represents the highest level of cultural development and is distinguished by the skill of writing, full-time specialized craftsmen, trade, cities, centralized political rule in the form of a state, and other characteristics made possible by the development of an agricultural surplus.

Cultures are always changing as societies adapt to new conditions. For example, the highest achievements of the pre-Columbian civilizations were destroyed by the Spaniards. Great cities like Tenochtitlán, ravaged by the conquistadors and rebuilt as Mexico City, supported a population of over one hundred thousand at the time of the conquest. The Spanish took over complex systems of law, government, taxation, and trade and adapted them for the exploitation of the native peoples. Indian art, science, and technology—which included elaborate systems of roads and irrigation works—gradually deteriorated and most of the aboriginal population of Latin America was reduced to an exploited peasantry. Some Indians were gathered into independent communities, where, under the protection of the Spanish crown, they continued to practice many folk customs. Thus, maize is still the staple food of the Latin American highland peasant today, much as in pre-Columbian times. These peasant communities, isolated from each other and from the national elite, were unable to sustain the high level of civilization reached under the Aztecs and the Incas.

Modern cultures, like cultures of the past, are always changing. Technological development, increasing interdependence of different segments of society, the spread of literacy, and the revolution in mass communication contribute to far more rapid change in modern societies. A major problem of anthropologists has been to devise a meaningful method of classifying these constantly changing and different cultures so that they provide a useful framework for understanding Latin America today.

The classifications have changed as the interests of anthropologists have shifted from a nearly exclusive concern with the pre-Columbian and primitive cultures of Latin America to the dynamics of change in contemporary Latin American society. The anthropologist in Latin America no longer confines himself to the study of the archaeological remains of Mayan civilization or to the study of primitive tribes in the Amazon basin. Now he studies peasants, plantation workers, the urban poor, and other contemporary groups of Latin American society.

In order to understand these groups the anthropologist must have a knowledge of the past because, while a culture is always changing, there is a continuity of cultural tradition over time. In the process of cultural change new ideas, techniques, and values are adopted as older patterns are discarded. New ideas are not borrowed indiscriminately. To be absorbed and integrated into the existing culture, innovations must be compatible with these older patterns; they must be reinterpreted to fit in with the existing value and behavior system. A classic ex-

AZTEC AND MAYA

PRIMITIVE HUNTERS AND GATHERERS

CHIBCHA

INCA

SOUTH AMERICA

MAIN CULTURE AREAS OF PRIMITIVE AMERICA

ample is the mass conversion of the Indians to Catholicism at the time of Spanish colonization. While the Indians consider themselves Catholics, and are so recognized by the Roman Catholic Church, they incorporated pre-Columbian pagan practices into their religious ritual and continue to follow these practices to the present day. In the mines of Bolivia, for example, the miners continue to make offerings to a man-made representative of the Devil in an Indian ritual known as *ch'alla*, which the miners feel will protect them from the hazards of this dangerous work.

In Latin America, until recently, the most obvious changes have occurred at the elite level of society: the rule of the Incas and Aztecs was replaced by that of the Spanish colonizers, who in turn were replaced by a national elite composed predominantly of large landowners. Most importantly, through all of these changes, the "folk" or nonelite segment of Latin American society remained essentially the same. It incorporated elements of the dominant elite culture but always retained a distinct way of life. Therefore, most studies by anthropologists have focused on this folk segment of Latin American society, which consists largely of a rural peasantry who follow a traditional way of life deeply tied to the soil.

## CONTEMPORARY CULTURE AREAS

This interest in the Latin American peasantry stimulated anthropologists to devote particular attention to the process by which the Indians incorporated elements of colonial Spanish tradition into their "folk" culture. The anthropologists focused on *acculturation*, or the process by which the subordinate group (in this case the Indians) interacts with the culture of the dominant group (in this case the Spanish—or Portuguese).

The interest in acculturation and in contemporary folk cultures fostered a new system of classifying Latin American cultures, differing considerably from the previous pre-Columbian focus. It still emphasized division into *culture areas* which are essentially geographic units in which similar cultures can be found. However, rather than classifying these cultures on the basis of the stage of cultural development, as was done in the case of the pre-Columbian culture areas, the boundaries of contemporary culture areas were determined by the strength of the dominant cultural tradition in each area.

Current scholars have also abandoned the earlier assumption that contemporary Latin American cultures could be classified into Indian and Spanish components. They did so because they realized that the cultures of the New World represented not just a combination of two separate cultural traditions, but a fusion which created a new cultural tradition quite distinct from either of its parent cultures. The process is analogous to trying to decide whether a child looks like his father or mother, when in reality he has inherited physical and psychological traits from both, but in a unique and distinct combination. As Indians are acculturated, they shed their tribal and indigenous way of life and become *mestizos*. Though strictly speaking, *mestizos* are persons of mixed Spanish and Indian ancestry, the term has a cultural as well as a biological meaning. Mestizos generally wear European dress, speak Spanish, and in other ways have adopted a more Western life-style.

Anthropologists, as a result of these new ideas, have classified Latin America into three major contemporary culture areas, the boundaries of which closely resemble the pre-Columbian areas. These culture areas clearly reflect the importance of the three major racial groups which have contributed to the development of Latin American society and culture: the aboriginal Indians, the black Africans, and the white Europeans.

1. *Indo-America or Mestizo America* comprises the highland Andean and Mesoamerica area of dense aboriginal population, where most of the natives still speak Indian languages, wear native costumes, and follow the diet, agricultural practices, and folk beliefs of their forebears. Because of the great degree of racial mixture in all but the most inaccessible areas, there are very few biologically "pure" Indians left.

2. *Afro-America or Plantation America* includes the Caribbean and most of the lowland coastal areas of Central and South America where the population is largely black or mulatto and the cultural heritage is predominantly African. The predominance of blacks in Afro-America resulted from the need for cheap labor on the highly profitable sugar plantations which flourished in the humid coastal lowlands, the islands of the

Caribbean, and in northeast Brazil. African slaves were imported in large numbers to replace the Indians, whose already sparse numbers were rapidly depleted through disease and enslavement by the colonists.

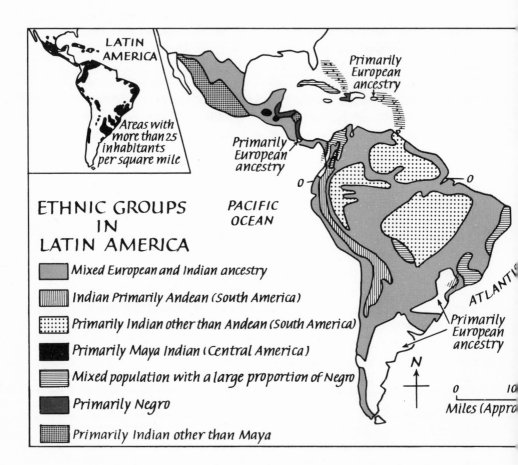

3. *Euro-America* encompasses areas such as Argentina, Uruguay, Chile, and Costa Rica, those areas of sparse aboriginal population that have been settled primarily by Europeans. Argentina in particular has been settled not only by Spaniards, but by immigrants from other European countries such as Italy and Germany in the late nineteenth and twentieth centuries.

The superiority of Spain in the colonization and exploitation of Latin America was challenged by the incursion of new European powers and by the move for political independence in most of the Latin American nations themselves. For the bulk of the rural population, independence from Spain primarily signified a change in the nature of the ruling elite. The hold of the Spanish bureaucracy maintained by the Spanish crown was broken and replaced by the far more personal and direct rule of the large landowners, who used their newfound political power to further their exploitation of the peasantry and to strengthen their economic hold over the countryside. The number of *haciendas* increased, while the number of independent Indian communities dwindled—particularly after the communal holdings were broken up and Indians were persuaded to sell off their individual property rights to the large landowners.

While the culture area concept is still a useful tool for organizing data or presenting course material on Latin America, the categories are too broad and general for purposes of analysis. There are so many differences within each of these areas, between city and country, between rich and poor, between highland and lowland, that it becomes necessary to think in terms of more specific categories within which contemporary Latin American cultures can be compared and grouped.

THE CONCEPT OF SUBCULTURE

To cope with these differences anthropologists have turned their attention to subcultures within Latin American society. A subculture represents the way of life of a segment of a society and may be defined on the basis of race, region, class, occupation, or any combination of these. For example, in Latin America, some of the more commonly recognized subcultures include the peasantry, the rural proletariat, and the urban proletariat. While peasants make their primary living from the land, the rural and urban proletariat depend completely on wages for their income. The rural proletariat work on plantations, usually located in warm, coastal areas where crops such as sugar cane, tobacco, cotton, coffee, and bananas thrive.

These subcultures can be found within each of the cultural areas described earlier. By using the subculture as the focus of analysis, the anthropologist is able more precisely to compare, for example, the rural proletariat on the plantations of the Caribbean with the rural proletariat of coastal Peru. The concept of subculture frees the anthropologist from the geographic boundaries imposed by the culture area concept and enables him to deal better with the increasing complexity of Latin American society.

The concept of subculture is also a useful device for analyzing change within Latin American society. New subcultures emerge in response to changing conditions, while old subcultures are modified and even eliminated. Many Indian subcultures in Latin America disappeared as the Indians became involved in a market and cash economy and therefore became peasants. Furthermore, many peasants have left the land to swell the ranks of the growing rural and urban proletariat.

## URBAN PROLETARIAT:
## AN EXAMPLE OF A SUBCULTURE

The urban proletariat, like the poor of our own cities, are an increasingly important segment of Latin American society. I will therefore discuss this group in some detail to serve as an example of a subculture.

The concentration of fertile land in the hands of large plantation owners, the increasing mechanization of agriculture, and the dramatic population growth have all increased the pressures on the peasantry to leave the land. In many areas, plots of land are now too small to support even an individual family. Some peasants have moved to new agricultural land opened up under government sponsorship in previously undeveloped areas, such as the settlement of the lowland regions in Peru and Bolivia. Many more, however, have moved to the cities, seeking a new source of income as unskilled wage laborers. When they make this move, the peasants become members of the fast-growing urban proletariat. The development of the squatter settlements in Latin America is in direct response to the large influx of rural migrants who have no other way of obtaining housing in the city. Private builders and government projects cannot cope with the needs of this rapidly swelling migrant population. The squatter settlement, or shanty town, is usually located on marginal land, often at the city's periphery, and is occupied illegally by squatters who build their own homes out of makeshift materials. The occupation of the land often takes place overnight. Frequently, the squatters are led by elected committees. Once the settlement is established, these committees assist the community in stimulating efforts at communal self-improvement, and in obtaining needed public services by bringing pressure to bear on politicians and public officials. Gradually, the squatter settlement may acquire roads, running water, electricity, schools, and other minimal public services. In time it begins to take on the characteristics of an established working class neighborhood and may be absorbed by the city proper.

In the Puerto Rican shanty town which I studied, most men worked on the docks, in construction, in factories, or at a variety of service jobs—unskilled, manual jobs offering little economic security and few opportunities for advancement. Most family incomes ranged under $3,000 a year, and a number of families, especially where the father was absent, depended on public welfare. They could afford few of the everyday comforts and pleasures that we take for granted, like meat every day, nice furniture and clothing, and toys for children. Their houses were often one room wooden shacks constructed of refuse lumber and tin. Sometimes these shanties were built on stilts over the polluted, reeking waters of a channel which serves as the main sewage outlet for the San Juan metropolitan area. While the government of the Commonwealth of Puerto Rico has conducted vigorous programs to eradicate these shanty towns and to relocate these families in public housing, a high percentage of the urban proletariat continue to live in miserable conditions.

Some people view the shanty towns as problems. Many others, including myself, see the shanty towns not as problems but as immediate solutions to pressing urban problems. Shanty towns provide the urban poor in Latin America with housing which they can afford and which they can improve as their resources increase. They also ease the adjustment of the rural migrant to urban life by providing him with a secure social setting in which there are familiar faces to whom he can turn for aid during this difficult transitional period. This arrangement occurs because the patterns of migration often follow kinship and village lines, and squatter settlements are composed of relatives and fellow villagers.

The important point is that city life, even in a shanty town,

A shantytown is home to this girl, and to many others like her. (*Mary Belfrage*)

seems to offer greater opportunity to the migrant than does his former rural environment.

## LOOKING AT THE FUTURE

In the view of many anthropologists, the single most important issue in contemporary Latin America is the struggle to incor-

This is the downtown of Santiago, capital city of Chile. The area in this photo is four blocks from *La Moneda*, the Presidential Palace. (*Batya Weinbaum—courtesy UNICEF*)

porate the subordinate peasant and proletariat subcultures into the mainstream of national life. Some progressive politicians agree and have turned their attention to these neglected groups. This is particularly true of Latin American countries that have experienced a national revolution, such as Mexico, Bolivia, and Cuba. As the peasants and the urban proletariat become more politically conscious and active, the demand increases for better public services and a more equitable distribution of resources. But in most Latin American countries, the peasantry and proletariat are still excluded from the national political process and treated as a subjugated, exploited labor force. The result is that for the most part their demands are not met. These groups remain largely powerless and they exercise little control over their own destinies. The challenge today in Latin America is: how can the peasantry and other subcultures be given a voice in the national political process? Is force necessary to end the duality of Latin American society and to achieve a modicum of well-being for people of all social levels?

The concept of subculture helps us to understand this challenge and the increasing diversification of Latin American society. It has taken us away from an exclusive concern with primitive peoples and pre-Columbian cultures or with culture areas and acculturation. As anthropologists focus on modern segments of society such as the urban or rural proletariat and concern themselves with current issues such as political power, land reform, or economic development, they force the other social sciences to pay more attention to the subordinate subcultures. These subcultures, always the traditional concern of anthropologists, still constitute the bulk of the Latin American population. We can no longer afford to neglect these oppressed subcultures. The Latin American people will no longer content itself with a mere change of political officials. They are demanding an end to the duality of Latin American society and a share in the benefits of material progress for all.

# 2: THE HISTORIAN'S PERSPECTIVE

## Samuel L. Baily

*Samuel L. Baily, Associate Professor of History at Rutgers University and author of several books on nationalism in Latin America, sets forth three characteristics of history which he believes determine the historian's perspective on Latin America: 1. the focus on the uniqueness of man and events; 2. the broad time perspective; and 3. the broad subject matter. His comments on the historian's time perspective might well be compared to Safa's discussion of continuity (Chapter 1), and his focus on the uniqueness of man should be compared with the ideas and assumptions of the three other social scientists on the uniformity of man. Baily concludes with a section on what history has to offer the person interested in Latin America today.*

THE HISTORIAN LOOKS AT LATIN AMERICA more or less in the same way he looks at any other area of the world, but the historian's perspective is distinct from that of the sociologist, economist, political scientist, philosopher, artist, or writer. The historian is similar to these social scientists and humanists in that his central concern is to understand man. He differs from the others in the aspects of man he chooses to write about, the assumptions he makes, the data he seeks, and the methods he uses. The purpose of this essay is to show how the historian looks at Latin America, or at any other area of the world, and to suggest what this perspective has to offer.

It is difficult to make generalizations about history and the historian's perspective because there are so many different kinds of history and there are such great philosophical and ideological differences among indivdual historians. The problem is further complicated by the fact that history is the only academic discipline that is both a social science and a humanity. To better understand the dual nature of history, let us look briefly at the development of the discipline during the past one hundred years.

Until the late nineteenth century, history was primarily a story, a record of the most important and dramatic events of human experience. The historian's emphasis was on narrative and style, and he wrote for the educated layman. History was a literary and humanistic art.

William H. Prescott was one of the great North American literary historians of the nineteenth century. In the following paragraph from his book *The Conquest of Mexico,* published in 1843, he is simply telling us that on November 8, 1519, Hernando Cortés and his men first set foot in the Aztec capital of Tenochtitlán (now Mexico City), but notice the use of poetic words and symbols and the use of imagination to set the mood for this important event:

With the first faint streak of dawn, the Spanish general was up, mustering his followers. They gathered, with beating hearts, under their respective banners, as the trumpet sent forth its spirit-stirring sounds across water and woodland, till they died away in distant echoes among the mountains. The sacred flames on the altars of numberless teocallis [temples], dimly seen through the grey mists of morning, indicated the site of the capital, till temple, tower, and palace were fully revealed in the glorious illumination which the sun, as he rose above the eastern barrier, poured over the beautiful Valley. It was the eighth of November, 1519; a conspicuous day in history, as that on which the Europeans first set foot in the capital of the Western World.

Most historians today do not cultivate the poetic insight and the artistic vision to the same degree as did Prescott, nor do they indulge in the use of historical imagination. But the literary humanistic tradition of history continues and historians still try to record the story of man with interest and excitement.

During the half-century preceding World War I, two things of significance influenced the writing of history. First, the professional historian, writing primarily for a professional audience, emerged. The major universities established professorships in history, and in 1884 a group of historians established the American Historical Association. Professional historians of Latin America emerged somewhat later than those in the more traditional fields of American and European history; the *Hispanic American Historical Review* was not established until 1918 and the Conference on Latin American History was not officially constituted as an associate body within the American Historical Association until 1928.

The emergence of the professional historian is important because he emphasized the discovery of new source material, the verification of data, and the interpretation and reinterpretation of events and individuals. He was interested in style, drama, and feeling only insofar as his source material permitted him to be. He was, in other words, more rigidly bound by his data and therefore less likely to use his imagination to fill in the information gaps.

The emergence of the professional historian was accompanied by the emergence of the social sciences—economics, political scence, anthropology, sociology, geography—and many historians were influenced by the social scientist's more precise methodology and his concern with the uniformities of man's

Machu Picchu, the lost city of the Incas. (*Samuel L. Baily*)

actions and thoughts. Since World War I and particularly since World War II, many historians have turned increasingly to the social sciences for new concepts and new methods with which to study man.

History thus is both a humanity and a social science. It has a humanistic, literary tradition which emphasizes the uniqueness of events, narrative description, drama, and the individuality of men. It also has been influenced by the concepts and methods of social science which emphasize uniformities, statistical analysis, predictability, and man in a statistical sense. The basic question is: given the fact that history is both a humanity and a social science, that there are varieties of history, and that there is considerable philosophical and ideological diversity among historians, is there anything common to all history which distinguishes it from other disciplines? Is there anything that we can reasonably identify as the historian's perspective?

My answer is yes, but this answer must be qualified. There are a number of *characteristics* which distinguish history from other disciplines, but these characteristics are not necessarily confined exclusively to history. Other disciplines may share with history one or more of these characteristics, but most historians place greater emphasis on all of these characteristics than do other scholars. *The emphasis on this particular cluster of characteristics constitutes the historian's perspective.*

## THE CHARACTERISTICS OF HISTORY

The first distinguishing characteristic of history is its focus on *the uniqueness of man and events.* Historians write biographies of leading personalities and monographs about specific crises and important developments. The historian makes the assumption that no two situations, no two events, no two processes, and no two individuals are exactly the same. He believes that the past is not, in any precise sense, repeatable, that the past can not be used to predict the future. Most historians assume that although man and events are to some degree comparable, they are essentially unique. They also believe that the focus on uniqueness separates history from the natural sciences and from those branches of the social sciences in which statistical generalizations and statistical prediction are the goals.

For example, historians have done a number of things with the Mexican Revolution which scholars from other disciplines have not. They have written biographies of Emiliano Zapata, Pancho Villa, Lázaro Cárdenas, and other leaders of the revolution, and have, for the most part, attributed greater importance to these individuals in determining the nature and course of this revolution than have political scientists and sociologists. They have also written about chance events (the assassination of Zapata in 1919) and unique documents (the Constitution of 1917) which they suggest have been decisive in the outcome of the revolution. Furthermore, although historians have compared the Mexican Revolution to the Bolivian, Cuban, and other revolutions and have pointed out similarities among these revolutions, they have insisted on the uniqueness of each. They have avoided analyses which, although they might relate things in one country to those in another, might also lead to a distortion of the situation in one place or the other. As a result, they have shied away from abstract models of revolution and from efforts to predict.

A corollary to the historian's assumption regarding the uniqueness of man and events in Latin America is his belief in *the importance of elites*. Traditionally, and to a considerable extent today, historians have focused on the individuals and groups at the top of the social, economic, and political hierarchies that appear to have determined the course of events. Historians looking at Latin America most often study conquistadors, viceroys, heroes of the Independence Movement, presidents, generals, landowners, revolutionary leaders, the upper classes, and the like. They do not, for the most part, study the anonymous Indian who fought against Cortés, the slave who worked the sugar plantations of Brazil and Cuba, the peon who lived and died on the *haciendas* of Mexico, the *gaucho* and the *llanero* (cowboy) who fought in the Independence Movements in Argentina and Venezuela, the Italian immigrants who swarmed over considerable parts of Latin America at the turn of the past century, the rank and file members of labor unions, and the dwellers in the shanty towns which surround almost all of the major Latin American cities today. This is so partly because there are so few data with which to study the nonelites in history, but it is also based on the assumption that the elites and the leading individuals in any group greatly influence the outcome of history and therefore deserve most of our attention. In recent years a few historians, particularly the young historians, have begun to study the Indian, the immigrant, the slave, and the worker, but for the most part historians still focus on the elites.

A second distinguishing characteristic of history is in *time perspective*. The historian sees man and events in the context of time, or in the context of all that has gone before and all that has happened since. He views Latin America or whatever specific aspect of it he is studying as one link in a long chain that stretches back farther than the Greeks and Romans and continues down to the present. He is seeking the traditions which affect subsequent events. He sees a continuity and a relationship among all of man's actions and thoughts.

Thus, for example, the historian studying race relations in Latin America today would begin with an analysis of Roman slavery. He would then examine the impact of Roman slavery, black Africans (Moors), and the Catholic Church on Spanish and Portuguese societies up to the time of the introduction of Negro slavery into the Americas (c. 1500). Next he would study the nearly four-hundred-year history of slavery in Spanish and Portuguese America and compare this system with those in the United States and in other parts of the New World. Finally, he would be ready to discuss the issues relating to race relations in contemporary Latin America: the attitudes of various races toward each other; the occupations, living standards, social positions, and political power of different races; the degree of assimilation of the groups involved; and the differences among race relations in various parts of Latin America and the Western Hemisphere.

On the ruins of the Inca city of Cuzco, the Spaniards built their churches. The Cathedral of Cuzco. (*Samuel L. Baily*)

The historian's treatment of widespread authoritarian political rule in Latin America offers us another example of his perspective. Again, the historian would begin his analysis by going back in time to medieval Iberia to examine the nature of political rule and specifically the nature of royal political power at that time. Next he would examine political rule in the Spanish and Portuguese colonies: the nature of imperialism, the viceroy system and its origins in Spain's Mediterranean empire, and the modifications of the system as it developed in the New World. He then would examine the Independence period and its impact on the nature of political rule, the development of the personalistic-authoritarian *caudillo* system of the nineteenth century, and finally the modifications—due to technological and ideological developments—of all these traditions in the twentieth century. He might then compare this tradition of political rule with that developed in other countries and other parts of the world.

In both of these examples the historian views his subject in the context of time, going back more than a thousand years in search of an evolving tradition which affects the nature of his subject. Without the knowledge of this tradition, he could not properly understand the subject.

A third distinguishing characteristic of history is its *broad subject matter*. Everything in the past, from the beginning of man to the present, is the domain of the historian, but I am not just referring to the social scientist's penchant to confine himself to present-day matters and the historian's willingness to delve into the past. The important point here is that the subject matter of history is all inclusive and that the historian is more willing than other social scientists to tackle certain kinds of issues regardless of their chronological position.

Scholars face the problem that they do not have adequate—let alone quantifiable—data or workable models with which to study many of the most important questions facing society (i.e., is capitalism or socialism the best way to develop Latin America; is political democracy compatible with development in Latin America; what is the impact of nationalism on Latin America?). Our choice is to ignore or postpone consideration of these questions or to utilize the available resources and concepts and proceed as best we can. The historian, who relies less than other social scientists on models and quantifiable data, is more willing to do the latter.

Let us look at the study of nationalism and the impact of nationalism on Latin America as an example. Most of us use the word "nationalism" and have some idea what it means. Many leading scholars of Latin America state categorically that nationalism is the most important single force operating in the area today, that it affects the acts of the governments and people of militarily governed Argentina and Brazil as much as those of revolutionary Mexico, Bolivia, and Cuba. Nevertheless, there is no agreement among these scholars on the definition of nationalism. There are a variety of definitions, but no one that is universally acceptable.

If we can not even agree upon a definition of nationalism, then how can we decide what is the relevant data and methodology for studying it, let alone talk about quantifying it? The idea is so influential that we simply accept the handicaps of lack of data and method, and proceed to study what we can. It is for this reason that historians have pioneered the study of nationalism in Latin America as elsewhere. They have, over the past half century, gathered information on specific manifestations of nationalism (i.e., the establishment of state-owned oil companies, the development of neutralist foreign policies, the reliance on native themes in literature) and have gradually begun to categorize and to generalize about the subject. More recently other social scientists, and in particular political scientists, have also begun to study nationalism, but the important point is that it was the historians who were willing to take on the task in the beginning when so little was known about the idea, thus encouraging others to study it.

Another dimension of broad subject matter is *the historian's role as synthesizer*. Because the historian sees all things related to man's actions and thoughts as his domain, he often acts as a synthesizer of the studies and works of many of the social sciences and humanities. The historian studying race relations in Latin America today must bring together a great deal of material from the past, as is mentioned above, but he will also utilize concepts and conclusions of the sociologist and the anthropologist, the insights from the plays and novels of the writer, and the analyses of the economist. Similarly, the historian studying nationalism must synthesize the writer's analysis of cultural identity, the economist's understanding of status income, the social psychologist's concepts regarding belonging and ultimate loyalty, and the political scientist's explanation of the legitimacy of the state. In both cases, the historian synthesizes the ideas of other scholars and incorporates the results into his own historical analysis of the subject.

## WHAT HISTORY OFFERS US

In recent years, many within and outside the profession have questioned history's relevance for man today. They raise such questions as: why study the past when there are so many pressing problems all around us today; why not study such contemporary-oriented subjects as sociology, political science, and economics rather than history; is there anything that is usable in the past?

One of the most perceptive critics of history is the young Princeton historian, Martin Duberman. In a recent book entitled *The Uncompleted Past*, Duberman argues that history cannot have any relevance for the present for two reasons: first, historians lack the necessary material which might enable them genuinely to understand the past; and second, each historical event is unique and therefore of no predictive value for the future.*

I agree with Duberman that each historical event is unique and that often we lack the data to re-create the past with a high degree of completeness. But does it then automatically follow that history has no relevance? I think not. I believe history is relevant in a variety of ways which I will set forth in the following paragraphs.

First of all, history offers us *a large body of specific knowledge* about ourselves. The historian combs the libraries, the newspapers, and the archives throughout the world in order to construct as accurately as possible the past of man. Most of what we know about the Spanish and Portuguese rule of Latin America has been dug up by historians. Much of the informa-

*Martin Duberman, *The Uncompleted Past* (New York: Random House, 1970).

The Indian markets are a living reminder of the past. The Indian market of Oaxaca. (*Samuel L. Baily*)

tion about Latin America which the political scientist, the economist, and the sociologist use has been located and recorded by historians. The historian has not been able to uncover as much information about the past as Duberman and others including myself might like, but this should not obscure the fact that historians have opened up massive amounts of material about our past.

Second, due to its broad time perspective, history is a *way of gaining experience* which will better enable us to understand ourselves. The past holds no *precise lessons* or formulas for action in the present or future as Duberman asserts. But knowledge of the past may well provide some *general lessons* for future action and may also provide a framework in which decisions might be better made.

The philosopher George Santayana clearly expressed the argument for the relevance of history by pointing out that "When experience is not retained, as among savages, infancy is perpetuated. Those who cannot remember the past are con-

demned to repeat it." Thus, for example, the study of slavery
in the Roman Empire, Spain, Brazil, and the United States in
conjunction with the study of race relations throughout the
world today will not produce specific means for avoiding or
ending a riot in Newark or Detroit, but it will help us understand the causes of such riots, how they relate to similar situations throughout history, and why black nationalism is so
powerful a force today. In this way the study of the past helps
us to respond more intelligently and humanely to such situations. The experience of history does not enable us to predict
in any precise sense, but it does help us to understand a situation after it has happened and may, in a general sense, help
us avoid repeating some of the errors of the past.

History also offers us *a sense of identity*. Through the study
of history we find out where we came from, who our ancestors
were, what our cultural tradition has been. We find our roots
in the past, we place ourselves within the continuum of history
or within the context of time, and in so doing we gain an
identity and a sense of belonging. We see that as part of the
continuous chain of men and events we are not alone. This
quest for identity is as old as man, from the most primitive
cave men who recorded their history with paint on the walls
of caves to the immigrants and the blacks of today who study
history to find their origins and identity.

Furthermore, history offers us *a breadth of view* that is particularly relevant in this age of increasing specialization. The
trend in scholarship today is to specialize, to write more and
more about less and less and to ignore the broad synthesis
or to leave it to others. Historians are more willing than other
social scientists to relate their subjects to broad sweeps of
history and to engage in the risky but necessary job of synthesis; they are more willing to study problems because the problems are important even if all of the data are not available or
not in the most convenient and complete form. Specialization
is important in any discipline, but what we do with the results
of specialized studies is the significant matter for the future
of man.

History also offers us a *certain kind of objectivity*. All people
—whether historians, sociologists, journalists, diplomats, brick-
layers, doctors, or ditch diggers—are to a greater or lesser

degree subjective in their evaluation of human events, either past or present. Yet when dealing with contemporary problems or more correctly with problems with which we are involved personally, we are more likely to be emotional and one-sided. If, however, we place the problem in the context of the past, as does the historian, we are encouraged to reach beyond our own immediate involvement to see more objectively the problem we are studying.

Latin America is also filled with large modern cities. Skyscrapers of São Paolo. (*Samuel L. Baily*)

For example, we may debate the justness and the value of imperialism, but if we study the great imperial empires of the past (the Roman, the Chinese, the Spanish, the Portuguese, the English), we can establish what we mean by imperialism, what some of its important characteristics are, and how the imperial system has affected the respective colonies and mother countries. Thus history can give us the objective criteria by which to define imperialism and its impact on the world, but it can not give us any objective criteria by which to evaluate the justness of imperialism, that is, to evaluate whether imperialism is a good thing or a bad thing.

And finally, history makes its knowledge, its experience, its sense of identity, its breadth of view, and its objectivity readily available to a large number of men. The historian for the most part makes use of less specialized jargon and methodology than any of the other social scientists and thus what he writes is more often intelligible to an educated person. The professional historian does often write primarily for his colleagues, but the humanistic tradition of history remains strong and much of this material is within the grasp of the educated citizen.

In conclusion let me reiterate that it is difficult to generalize about the nature of history and of historians, and certainly not all historians would agree with what I have written. I have set forth what I believe are some of the most important characteristics of the discipline: the focus on the uniqueness of man and events, the broad time perspective, and the broad subject matter. The particular emphasis on these characteristics constitutes the historian's perspective whether he is looking at Latin America or some other area, and this perspective offers a great deal to modern man.

# 3: ECONOMIC ISSUES IN A GROWING LATIN AMERICA

## James H. Street

*James H. Street, Professor of Economics at Rutgers University and author of several studies on the problems of growth in Latin America, begins his essay with a discussion of sporadic industrialization, the population explosion, and other causes of Latin America's current economic problems and disorders. He then examines the Latin Americans' efforts to modernize their economies and to achieve a higher standard of living; he presents the views of two opposing schools of economists—the monetarists and the structuralists—on these issues. He analyzes the important theory of comparative advantage and the doctrine of free trade upon which it is based, import substitution, and inflation. His dual economy is clearly related to Safa's dual society (Chapter 1) and his comments on the issue of standard of living are similar to those of Turner (Chapter 4), but his call for more scientific research to increase agricultural productivity seems to conflict with the ideas expressed by Bazin (Chapter 5). Street concludes that the economists' realization of the complexity of the problems they face and the movement away from rigid doctrinaire positions provide some hope for the future.*

LATIN AMERICA IS NOW experiencing turbulent and rapid growth comparable to the dramatic internal expansion that took place in the United States a century ago. The population is growing faster there than in any other area of the world. Cities with their shanty towns are mushrooming all over the continent. New factories, railroads, steel mills, highways, automobile assembly plants, and oil refineries are sprouting almost everywhere from Mexico to Argentina. A class of urban business executives, government officials, engineers, and accountants is rising to manage these new industries. Hundreds of thousands of workers are streaming into the cities to meet the increased demand for industrial labor.

This growth is producing serious problems which Latin Americans are attempting to understand and solve. While some anthropologists are focusing on the social problems of living under urban conditions and many political scientists are looking at the changing power relationships among the new groups, the economists are concerned with how to increase and how to distribute the resources of their societies. The human and physical resources of Latin America are limited and the demand for them is both rising and changing. In other words, the demand for more and different goods and services is outpacing their production. Therefore, the primary concern of the economists is to examine and offer solutions to the problems arising from the conflict between the existing resources and the changing demands.

More specifically, the economists focus on two sets of questions. First, how does a country increase its output of goods and services? To support industrial growth should it borrow money from another country or should it raise funds internally? Should it seek expert, technical knowledge from abroad or should it concentrate on developing its own technicians? Should it support a revolution aimed at destroying the power of the landowners if they oppose industrialization? Second, how should a country distribute its increased goods and services among the people? Should it immediately produce consumer goods such as refrigerators and transistor radios or should it build up its heavy industries for the manufacturing of steel and railroad cars? Should it pay high wages so that people can buy more goods or should it hold down wages in an effort to save money for investment? Should it primarily tax the consumer on his purchases, or the landowner on his land, or the corporations on their factories and stores? Should it protect domestic industries with high tariffs from foreign competition?

While economists disagree on the answers to these and other questions, they do agree that all in all the economic growth of Latin America gives every appearance of being uncontrolled and undirected. But before presenting the disagreements on these questions and the proposed solutions for bringing order to the economy let us look at the economic development of Latin America in an historical perspective.

## THE HISTORY OF ECONOMIC DEVELOPMENT

Many of the present economic difficulties of Latin America are rooted in its past. When the Latin American republics obtained their independence from Spain and Portugal during the nineteenth century, most of them continued the economic way of life of the past four or five centuries. A considerable number of people, especially in Middle America and the Andean countries, continued to live in mountain villages and the colonial *hacienda,* the feudal plantation of the wealthy landowners. In their isolation, the peasants pursued a life of self-sufficiency, using old methods of agriculture. They farmed their patches of corn, beans, and potatoes with primitive tools much in the manner of their Aztec, Mayan, and Incan forbears.

In the more advanced areas, those in touch with the outside world, the former Spanish and Portuguese overlords were replaced by landlords and employers born in the New World. These new Latin American leaders were imbued with feelings of national independence and personal ambition. Yet these leaders generally perpetuated the institutions of the past. On large plantations they produced foodstuffs and raw materials for export. Land was the chief form of investment. Labor was organized under an arrangement whereby the tenants worked the property of the landlord and in addition gave strong personal, political, and military support to him. In return they received protection and care in the form of minimal wages, food, clothing, and shelter, and an occasional favor.

Modern technology did not take root in this kind of economic structure because there was an abundance of low-paid workers and therefore little reason to introduce laborsaving machines. Yet trade with the rest of the world expanded based on such traditional products as coffee, sugar, rubber, silver, and guano (bird manure used for nitrates).

Toward the end of the last century European and North American businessmen looked for new opportunities and large

Industrialization notwithstanding, the old ways to do things go on. Transportation of goods in this Ecuadorian town is done by human burro. (*Mary Belfrage*)

profits in the great Latin American frontier. Their investments began to change the traditional economic structure. These large foreign investments led to outside financial control, outside managerial direction, and the introduction of some modern technology. In this way England and the United States replaced Spain and Portugal as the main foreign influence on the Latin American economy.

A technological explosion stimulated by foreign investments began in Argentina around 1870. European businessmen built large packing plants and grain elevators to prepare Argentine beef and wheat for export. They installed a railroad network to transport cattle and wheat from the fertile pampas to the ports. They dredged the silted estuary of the Rio de la Plata at Buenos Aires and the interior city of Rosario to permit ocean-going vessels to reach dockside. These were enormous engineering undertakings for their time. British yards supplied most of the shipping. As a result of improvements in meat processing and carefully controlled refrigeration on the long voyage, fine Argentine beef arrived in the European markets in nearly fresh condition where it was sold at a premium price.

These and other technological innovations, together with the managerial skill to use them, transformed Argentina. Where Argentina was formerly an isolated, culturally dormant hinterland it became a modern nation in direct contact with the most advanced countries of the world. Buenos Aires became a throbbing commercial and cultural center.

Other Latin American countries developed similarly. Deposits of silver, lead, and zinc in Mexico, nitrates and copper in Peru and Chile, and petroleum in Venezuela also attracted foreign businessmen. For the first time the precipitous slopes of the Andes were mounted by twisting railways, power lines, and telegraph poles to serve the new industrial undertakings. In the tropical zones of Central America and Brazil foreign businessmen built railroads and modern shipping facilities to serve the recently developed sugar, banana, and coffee plantations.

During this period (around 1900) Latin America developed a dual economy. The cities became centers of trade and industry. They were linked to overseas markets and controlled to a considerable degree by foreign investors. The urban economy was directly affected by foreign wars, depressions, and rivalries

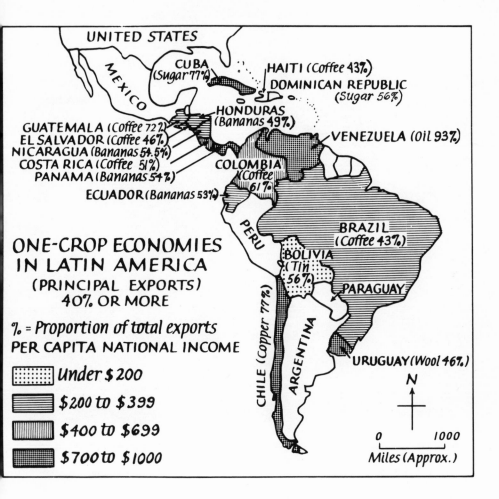

UNITED STATES

MEXICO

CUBA
(Sugar 77%)

HAITI (Coffee 43%)
DOMINICAN REPUBLIC
(Sugar 56%)

HONDURAS
(Bananas 49%)

GUATEMALA (Coffee 72%)
EL SALVADOR (Coffee 46%)
NICARAGUA (Bananas 54.5%)
COSTA RICA (Coffee 51%)
PANAMA (Bananas 54%)

ECUADOR (Bananas 53%)

VENEZUELA (Oil 93%)

COLOMBIA
(Coffee 61%)

PERU

BRAZIL
(Coffee 43%)

BOLIVIA
(Tin 56%)

PARAGUAY

CHILE (Copper 77%)

ARGENTINA

URUGUAY (Wool 46%)

**ONE-CROP ECONOMIES
IN LATIN AMERICA**
(PRINCIPAL EXPORTS)
40% OR MORE

% = *Proportion of total exports*
PER CAPITA NATIONAL INCOME

*Under $200*

*$200 to $399*

*$400 to $699*

*$700 to $1000*

N

0        1000
Miles (Approx.)

among the powerful nations. However, the remote areas of the interior remained largely the same since the new technology did not penetrate to them. For the most part they continued as self-sufficient economic units steeped in their traditional agricultural ways. They were stable and undisturbed by outside events. Throughout Latin America the dual economy set the cities apart from the countryside and set the landowners and businessmen apart from the village peasants, plantation workers, and miners.

As a result of the commercial and industrial development in the cities two new groups of people emerged: the middle

This photograph was taken in Rio Bueno, Chile, where women learn to use sewing machines. Women use the center facilities to make clothes for themselves and their families and also for sale in the marketplace. (*Batya Weinbaum—courtesy UNICEF*)

class and the lower working class. The middle class was made up of native and immigrant shopkeepers, government employees, owners and managers of small factories, and office workers. The urban lower class was made up of native and immigrant workers in construction, shipping, factories, and transportation.

These groups introduced new political and economic ideas. From the economist's point of view the most important was the desire for economic independence for Latin America. Mexico took the lead in the late 1930's in establishing economic independence by seizing the foreign-owned oil properties and placing them under the direction of a government-owned oil corporation, PEMEX (*Petroleos de Mexico*). As other Latin American countries followed suit by nationalizing railroads, power plants, telephones and telegraph systems, petroleum industries, and even some manufacturing plants, they met with serious problems. For example, they found that there was a shortage of native managers and technicians with sufficient experience to manage the newly nationalized industries.

In addition to the problems arising from domination by foreign businessmen and later efforts to achieve economic independence, Latin America also met with economic difficulties due to the growth and redistribution of population. The successful campaigns to eliminate such killer diseases as malaria and yellow fever sharply reduced the death rate. At the same time the high birth rate remained essentially the same, which resulted in a dramatic gain in population. Furthermore, there was a major shift in population from the rural areas to the cities. Demographers predict that Latin America, which had about 200 million people in 1960, will reach a population triple that size by the end of the century. By that time it is expected that the Caracas-Maracaibo metropolitan zone of Venezuela will contain 50 million people and the area surrounding the city of São Paulo, Brazil, will comprise a megalopolis of 80 million (more than one-third the present population of the United States). It is hard to imagine how such numbers will be absorbed productively in those admittedly rich zones, much less in areas with fewer resources.

## INTERPRETATIONS OF THE GROWTH PROCESS

In response to the changes brought by industrial penetration and rapid population growth, Latin Americans have developed an almost universal desire for modernization and economic advancement. A number of economists have proposed various routes to achieve a higher standard of living for the general population. The two most important alternatives are those of the "monetarists" and the "structuralists." The monetarists emphasize the role of free market forces in regulating the economy. They believe that countries grow best when there is a minimum of intervention by government in planning and promoting industry. This task is best accomplished by private businessmen who pursue their own opportunities in response to what consumers will buy. Also the monetarists believe that industry operates more successfully when it uses private funds and is under private control than when it is owned and operated by the government. The proper role of the government, according to the monetarists, is to create a favorable climate for private investment by following conservative policies in spending government funds and in issuing paper money.

The monetarists are closely associated with official U.S. policy and with leading international financial organizations such as the International Monetary Fund (IMF) and the World Bank.

The structuralists emphasize government intervention into the economy as a means of stimulating industrial growth. While not necessarily supporting the ownership and control of industry by the government (as do most socialists), the structuralists believe that extensive central planning is necessary to promote development. In general, they support looser money creation and a larger use of government loans and subsidies than do the monetarists. The structuralists advocate strong measures by government to overcome backwardness in farming and to foster the growth of new industries, even if this means redistribution of land, increasing resort to tariff protection, and direct government investment in factories.

The structuralists are closely associated with the United Nations Economic Commission on Latin America (ECLA) and particularly with the ideas of ECLA's former director, Raúl Prebisch.

Let us look at each of these two alternative economic schools of thought in greater detail.

### a. The Monetarists' Case

Monetarists look favorably on foreign trade and private investment as the principal means by which poor countries can participate in the prosperity of rich industrial countries. Poor countries can do this in two ways: by using foreign trade to raise the domestic level of consumption; and by using foreign investment to obtain more industrial equipment for increasingly diversified production.

The principle of international specialization and exchange (known as the theory of comparative advantage) permits any country to enjoy a higher standard of living through specialization. Each country specializes in producing those goods that its resources allow, and exchanges the resulting surplus products for those of other countries similarly specializing in *their* most favorably produced goods. In its simplest terms, the theory of comparative advantage states that if each country does what it can do best, all will benefit in trade.

For example, it was only a matter of common sense for late-nineteenth-century Argentina, with its extensive land space, sparse population, and rudimentary industry, to specialize in the production of meat, wheat, and wool and to send these products to England in exchange for British manufactured goods. By this means Argentines lived better than if they had tried to supply all their own needs at home. Such an arrangement demanded free trade, unhampered by tariffs or other economic restrictions. Indeed, in the initial stage of her growth, the system worked very well for Argentina, as well as for her principal partner, England.

Furthermore, according to the monetarists, the less developed countries can take advantage of the industrial methods of the advanced countries through the tools and machines supplied by private investors. Skilled and imaginative businessmen seeking profit opportunities in new lands can introduce the benefits of modern technology and managerial organization, can help to develop the national economies, and can create local sources of employment. These ideas were borne out when skilled European and North American engineers and workmen were attracted by the opportunities created in the industrializing New World.

### b. *The Structuralists' Case*

The structuralists argue that the theory of comparative advantage has not worked to the advantage of the general Latin American population. Therefore, they propose that the governments intervene to develop their economies from within. Using trade statistics, Raúl Prebisch, the former director of ECLA, tries to show that less developed countries which mainly export raw materials and foodstuffs have suffered a long-term disadvantage by trading with the countries producing manufactured goods. For example, if an Argentine farmer had been able to buy an imported tractor in 1931 for the value of 500 bushels of his exported wheat, Prebisch believes that it has taken more and more wheat to buy a similar tractor in succeeding years.

Prebisch attributes this decline in the *real* terms of trade to the fact that Argentine wheat growers, using traditional methods, were unable to lower their costs of production very much, while tractor manufacturers in the industrial countries had the increasing benefits of mass production and lower unit costs. However, instead of passing on their lower costs in the form of lower prices, the industrial countries learned to cut back production and maintain relatively high prices. On the other hand, agricultural countries were forced to accept the declining prices because of periodic overproduction and dependence on a few traditional products.

Prebisch and his ECLA colleagues also argue that international private investment has failed to stimulate diversified industrialization in the less developed countries. This is so because such private investment has tended to be concentrated in a few export industries, such as mining and petroleum production, and has not spread its influence to other industries. For example, the formerly American-owned Kennecott and Anaconda copper companies used extremely modern mining equipment to extract copper in Chile without significantly affecting the rest of the economy. In spite of the improvements in the foreign-owned companies, the Latin American–owned industries have not modernized. Therefore, foreign investment and the free market economy have reinforced the dual economy and widened the divisions between social classes.

The structuralists also claim that though the theory of comparative advantage might have served a purpose in the early stages of Latin American development, it no longer works. Today the comparative advantage theory condemns Latin America to worsening relations with the industrialized countries. The structuralists view the theory of comparative advantage as *static* and therefore not applicable to the *dynamic* growth of Latin America today.*

## c. *The Counter-Arguments*

The monetarists have responded to the structuralists' argument by questioning Raúl Prebisch's statistics. They point out that his statistics do not take into account the quality improvements that industrial producers constantly make in their manufactured goods. A bushel of wheat produced in Argentina in 1971 is virtually the same as the wheat produced in 1931. But a 1971 American tractor is a vastly improved piece of equipment compared to one produced forty years earlier. In other words, though the farmer needs more bushels of wheat to pay for a new tractor, he receives a much better tractor, which helps him grow more wheat. Hence, the monetarists argue, the real terms of trade may actually have improved for Argentina during this period.

The monetarists also claim that the terms of trade have not declined for all products and all countries. What has happened to coffee or cotton has not happened to all other products of Latin America. The prices of tin, copper, silver, and petroleum

*At one time the structuralists proposed another policy called "import substitution." Under import substitution the Latin American countries would try to increase the variety of their own industrial products by providing tariff protection for home manufacturers of goods that had previously been imported. Instead of importing steel, cloth, automobiles, and drugs, each country would try to produce these articles at home. This is a policy for the support of infant industries much like that proposed by Alexander Hamilton in his "Report on Manufactures" in our early history.

The import substitution policy is no longer strongly supported because of the difficulty of making it work. Markets in most of the Latin American countries are as yet so small that it is difficult for domestic companies in their infancy to reach a large enough size to achieve the benefits of mass production techniques even though heavily protected by such things as tariffs. As a result, foreign products from the industrially advanced countries still come in over the protective barriers. Also, many of the new industries use raw materials such as plastics and synthetic fibers that are not produced domestically. Therefore the demand for imports merely shifts from finished goods to raw materials that may be just as hard to pay for. Moreover, when a country fails to earn enough on its exports to pay for the new raw materials, its infant industries may be forced to shut down.

have risen sharply at times when there has been strong demand for them in foreign industrial countries. Some Latin American countries have enjoyed good earnings while others have not.

The structuralists react by pointing out that the "one-product" economy of most Latin American countries remains unfavorable to them. The uncertainties faced by these countries are real indeed. Because of changes in weather conditions, rarely are the agricultural countries able to control the supply of coffee, sugar, wheat, and other products that they export. Even the mineral-producing countries suffer from their inability to control their income since the prices they receive are set in foreign markets.

In any case, the argument has shifted recently from Raúl Prebisch's claim about the "worsening terms of trade" to a general agreement that what hurts Latin American countries most is the uncertainty of their income from foreign trade from year to year. The structuralists say it is impossible to plan a long-range development program when a country's foreign earnings go up sharply one year and down the next. The monetarists agree that such fluctuations are unsettling, but believe they are best handled by frequent adjustments (devaluations) in the international value of a country's money and by temporary loans to tide the country over during difficult periods. As a result, the International Monetary Fund has loosened its regulations and permits its members to borrow during emergencies of this type.

## INTERPRETATIONS OVER PERSISTENT INFLATION

As part of their disagreements over growth processes, the monetarists and structuralists also differ regarding the question of persistent inflation. Constant increases in the cost of living in which prices have often risen more than 20 percent year after year have been typical in many Latin American countries recently. This inflation has affected the more economically advanced countries such as Argentina, Brazil, Chile, and Uruguay as well as less advanced countries like Bolivia and Peru.

## a. *The Monetarists' Case*

The monetarists blame persistent inflation on irresponsible governments that spend more than they have and make up the difference by merely printing additional paper money. They believe that the only effective solution for inflation is a policy of austerity, or "belt tightening." They propose that a government should reduce spending, raise taxes, and limit the issuing of new money. Under this policy businessmen and consumers would be forced to limit their purchases because their incomes would level off. As a result of decreased spending, prices would cease to rise and become stabilized.

Austerity programs were the policy of several Latin American countries during the 1950's when they suffered their sharpest inflation. Foreign bankers, foreign governments, and experts from the International Monetary Fund recommended this policy. They were able to enforce their recommendations for austerity by denying outside aid to the countries which did not follow their advice.

In some cases the austerity programs were highly successful; in others, they had only a temporary effect. Peru's relatively mild inflation was effectively stopped in the early fifties, and Bolivia's wild runaway of prices shortly thereafter was arrested by drastic measures in 1957. Chile, which has suffered a chronic rise in the cost of living for nearly a century, experienced a price explosion in 1953 that reached a yearly inflation rate of over 80 percent by 1955. The following year the government applied a severe anti-inflation program that brought the rate of inflation down to 17 percent by 1957. Unemployment rose sharply, however, and a sudden drop in the price of copper, Chile's principal export, contributed to the abandonment of the stabilization program the following year. Repeated efforts have been made since then to curb price rises.

Brazil had an exhilarating experience in the 1950's and early 1960's when inflation seemed to contribute to rapid industrialization and a high rate of economic growth. However, by 1964 the inflation had gotten out of control and threatened to double the cost of living in one year. The government of President João Goulart was overthrown by a conservative military group who applied an austerity program that slowed the inflation considerably without completely eliminating it.

Argentina has also had a long experience with inflation. Various government administrations have applied the monetary brakes from time to time, successfully slowing the price rise in 1960 and 1969, but austerity has never been tolerated by the powerful labor unions for very long. They insist that the burden of stabilization programs always falls most heavily on the working class because prices continue to go up while wages are frozen.

Monetarists point out that it is not the stabilization programs that are to blame but the inflation itself, which operates very unevenly and cruelly to reward speculators and hoarders with higher incomes, while it hurts the weaker members of society. They assert that if the austerity programs were only carried on long enough to become effective, then the inequities that inflation tends to emphasize would be eliminated.

Monetarists also attach importance to the secondary effects of inflation: it discourages domestic saving and causes local investors to send their funds abroad for a more secure return, thus reducing the amounts available for investment in home industry. Inflation also tends to worsen a country's balance of payments and cause its money to decline in value relative to other countries' currencies. Because it raises domestic costs of production, inflation makes it harder for a country to export. All of these maladies, according to the monetarists, result from unwise monetary expansion and can be cured only by reversing the process.

b. *The Structuralists' Case*

The case of the structuralists is based on a different explanation of the causes of inflation. The structuralists believe that inflation results from several "structural bottlenecks," or obstructions to the growth process. Some of the bottlenecks are (1) inadequate export earnings, (2) sluggish farm production, (3) small domestic markets, (4) ineffective tax systems, and (5) the population explosion. When one or more of these bottlenecks blocks the normal process of economic growth, pressure builds up on the government to correct the problem and the method applied usually involves increased government spending; hence, inflation. Let us see how these bottlenecks operate.

The first bottleneck is inadequate export earnings. We can imagine that a Latin American country is growing satisfactorily, using a portion of its income from the sale of export products to buy machinery for its expanding industries. If Latin America suffers from a gradual worsening of the terms of trade, as Prebisch believes, or even if there is only a sharp temporary drop in export earnings, the country affected finds that its income falls and some of its own people are thrown out of work. Machinery is harder to import. People turn to their government for financial assistance and excessive spending begins.

The situation becomes even worse when we consider that few Latin American countries produce all the goods their consumers want to buy, and a portion of the earnings from exports has to be reserved for imported products. Each year the people of Latin America become acquainted with and want a wider variety of products: nylon stockings, transistor radios, Coca Cola, foreign movies, and antibiotic drugs. A decline in export earnings means that these imports become scarcer and more expensive.

Of course, a country may borrow from foreign banks to meet a temporary shortage of income, but this has been done so often that most of the Latin American countries now have a large debt burden hanging over them. This debt becomes hopelessly difficult to pay off, say the structuralists, just because of the export bottleneck. Until the countries can overcome their dependence on traditional exports and diversify, they must depend more and more on their internal resources.

This is where the second bottleneck comes into play: the sluggishness of domestic agriculture. Latin America is growing in population, and as it industrializes, its people move to the cities to escape rural poverty and to look for jobs. If those who remained on the farm were progressive and produced sufficient surpluses, the growing urban population could be fed without a rise in the cost of food. As it is, the traditional system of landholding, limited education, and antiquated methods of farming combine to make farmers very unresponsive to urban needs. Food prices go up in the cities, and the government, unwilling to disturb the powerful landowning class, meets the rising cost of living with officially approved wage increases.

The third bottleneck also concerns domestic production. In order to reduce their dependence on imported consumer goods, we have noted that many Latin American countries have resorted to the process called "import substitution." They have encouraged the creation of new industries to produce goods formerly imported. Government leaders recognize that at the beginning these industries have to be sheltered from established foreign producers by tariff walls and sometimes by government subsidies. However, it is expected that in time these infant industries will grow strong enough to stand on their own feet and to compete effectively in domestic markets.

The bottleneck that has made this difficult is the smallness of domestic markets. Unless automobile and electric appliance factories can sell a large volume of goods, they have a hard time getting their costs down to levels competitive with the large producers in West Germany, Japan, and the United States. In Latin America rarely is this possible. That is why the structuralists have given so much attention to the formation of a Latin American Common Market which would enlarge the opportunities for local producers to sell to their neighbors within the region.

Another way to expand the market for domestic industries, according to the structuralists, would be to reduce the great differences of income between the few very rich people and the many poor in Latin America. This has been accomplished to a considerable degree in Western Europe and the United States through the graduated income tax combined with an extensive social security system. Raising the incomes of the poor would expand the sales opportunities for local producers of consumer goods.

What stands in the way is the bottleneck of an ineffective tax system. Wealthy Latin Americans simply do not pay their income and inheritance taxes no matter what the tax laws say. Hence, the government is forced to rely on sales taxes and import duties, both of which raise the cost of living. Tax reform, say the structuralists, is essential to a reduction of inflation.

Finally, the bottleneck that intensifies all of the other problems is the rapid upsurge in population growth that has been occurring in Latin America in the last half century. More population means more mouths to feed and more city dwellers to supply with the needs of modern urban life. Even if the birth rate levels off, the rising number of young adults in this generation will insure a phenomenal rise in population during the remainder of this century.

In their running argument with the monetarists, the structuralists concede that Latin American governments have often been irresponsible, that they have issued too much paper money and spent more than tax collections would justify. However, they believe that in light of the present difficult circumstances

A day care class of four-year-olds (La Nueva Havana, Chile) staffed by university students and community volunteers. The community (*campamiento*) locates a useable building and the government provides funds for books and buses. (*Batya Weinbaum–courtesy UNICEF*)

Outside Cuenca, Ecuador, we see an example of home manufacturing, or cottage industry. This woman is at home making "Panama" hats which she will sell to an exporter. (*Batya Weinbaum–courtesy UNICEF*)

even the best of governments has little choice but to respond both to the pressures created by the bottlenecks and to the political parties that represent the affected groups. They accuse the monetarists of fixing their attention too narrowly on the connection between money and inflation. They say the monetarists are unwilling to recognize that until the bottlenecks are eliminated no government can maintain a stable monetary and fiscal policy. Moreover, they charge that conservative monetary policies prevent Latin American businessmen from obtaining the funds they need for industrial expansion and farmers from receiving the credit they need for modernization. Austerity programs, they say, strangle growth, and without growth inflation will never be overcome.

In summary, while structural economists have not united behind a common program, most would support the following measures to relieve the bottlenecks: the stimulation of nontraditional exports and the formation of a Latin American Common Market to alleviate inadequate export earnings; land reform and rural education to overcome the sluggishness of agriculture; and tax reform and redistribution of income to enlarge domestic markets. They are not fully agreed as to what to do about the rapid growth of population, as many Latin Americans believe that the region has ample room to absorb a larger population if only enough jobs can be created. However, the subjects of family planning and population control are now being openly discussed in Latin America as they never were before.

## CONCLUSION

In the heat of the argument between the monetarists and structuralists needlessly rigid positions were taken by each side. For a time the policies of the United States government and the International Monetary Fund (IMF) were almost indistinguishable from those of the most conservative, backward-looking elements in Latin American society, while the Economic Commission on Latin America (ECLA) and the structuralists represented the liberal, interventionist forces and were often painted as wildly radical. Recently the IMF has modified its policies to give more support to countries with balance-of-payments problems resulting from a fall in the price of traditional exports such as coffee. The Fund's experts now seem more willing to recognize the region's growth needs as well as the need for stability. Under the Alliance for Progress program begun in 1961 by President John F. Kennedy, the United States also showed more sympathy for the structural imbalances of Latin America, helping to finance improvements in farming, transportation, schools, and living conditions. Under the administration of President Richard M. Nixon foreign aid has been reduced, but President Nixon has offered to reduce tariffs on Latin American manufactured goods.

At the same time, the structuralists have retreated from earlier extreme positions. Most of them no longer believe in a deliberate policy of inflation as a good way to promote economic growth, and some have been disappointed with the efforts to apply import substitution that they had formerly supported. Each side of the conflict that we have reviewed is now perhaps ready to concede that the problems of Latin American development are stubbornly difficult and that it will take all the fresh ideas available to cope with them. Trade and balance-of-payments problems still persist, and the rising cost of living is a constant threat throughout the region.

What we are seeing in Latin America, as we said at the beginning, is a region and a group of peoples experiencing a stormy growth process for which there are no boundaries or guidelines. That there has been a vast improvement in general health and living conditions is evident when one compares modern Latin America with its recent past. Latin America is still in many ways an undeveloped frontier. This poses a challenge for the economist: can he find ways to reduce the pain of rapid social change and help to make the growth of the region a more humane and orderly process?

# 4. ATTITUDES AND STRATEGIES IN LATIN AMERICAN POLITICS

## Frederick C. Turner

*Frederick C. Turner, Professor of Political Science at the University of Connecticut and author of several books on nationalism and on the Church in Latin America, begins his essay by discussing two basic concepts of political science—power and influence. He then raises the issues of the citizen's relationship to his government, the nature of political groups, and the relationship of violence and social change, all in the context of Latin American politics. His discussion of the individual's rights might well be compared to similar discussions by Street (Chapter 3) and Safa (Chapter 1), and his statement that political science incorporates the concepts and findings of other social sciences should be compared to Baily's (Chapter 2) statement regarding history as synthesizer. Professor Turner concludes by examining the role of the United States in the development of Latin America and asks: "By what criteria do North Americans decide whether or not they should promote their ideology and their political institutions in Latin America, or when and to what extent they should promote them?"*

POLITICAL SCIENCE IS A NORTH AMERICAN DISCIPLINE that is being increasingly used to study the political realities of Latin America. Besides developing concepts and techniques of its own, it freely borrows from the conclusions and the tools of analysis of other disciplines such as history, sociology, anthropology, and psychology. It concentrates on the issue of *power* and *influence,* asking questions about how governments, institutions, and citizens behave, how they could behave more ethically and more effectively, and how conflicts of interest among them can best be resolved. A major strength of this discipline has been its flexibility, its willingness to test many hypotheses and to accept many approaches in attempting to answer the basic questions which it raises.

Political scientists use a wide variety of techniques to study issues which deal with the political behavior and attitudes of citizens, groups, and governments. Traditional political theory asks what are the morally just goals and strategies of political activity, while newer lines of theory have become more "empirical" in the sense that they establish models or detailed patterns through which political relationships are expected to occur, and then test the models against real experiences to see to what extent the relationships actually occur in the expected ways. All political science is comparative, but particular approaches apply best in specific political contexts. Personal interviews and written questionnaires measure and contrast the views and backgrounds of congressmen, students, or blue-collar workers, while analysis of voting patterns reveals power relationships and trends in California, or in France, or in the United Nations General Assembly. The use of questionnaires or voting analysis is not possible in an authoritarian country like Communist China, however, and here political scientists must rely on such traditional sources of information as written documents and personal observation.

The study of Latin America from the perspective of political science is relatively recent. As a discipline which has evolved chiefly in the United States during the twentieth century, political science has concentrated much more on the United States and Western Europe than on Latin America, Africa, or Asia. While some political scientists have studied Latin America for decades, the rise of Fidel Castro and apparent threats to United States interests have more recently increased attention among other scholars as well as among government officials. Comparatively few Latin Americans understand that political science is a discipline separate from history, law, or constitutional interpretation, so that political scientists working in Latin America often identify themselves as sociologists in order to make their interests more readily understood. Gradually, however, with the founding of political science faculties in such cities as Rio de Janeiro, Buenos Aires, and Santiago de Chile, Latin Americans themselves are coming more and more to apply the framework and questions of this discipline to their own situations.

The present essay takes up some of the issues with which political scientists deal, illustrates parts of their methodology, and does so in the context of Latin American politics. The essay explains how political scientists now look at Latin America—but students should not be content simply with seeing what the present perspective is. Like political scientists themselves, they should go on to ask how the perspective and the methods of this discipline should be modified in the future so that we can more adequately understand the realities of power and influence.

## THE CITIZEN'S VISION OF HIS RELATIONSHIP TO GOVERNMENT

One of the major issues in political science deals with how citizens relate to their government. Are they aware of what elected officials and government agencies do at the national, state, and local levels, and do they distinguish between the ways in which their government affects them and the ways in which they can in turn affect their government? What attitudes do citizens have toward government programs, and what differences exist among the attitudes and perceptions of different groups in the society? While political scientists have traditionally tried to answer such questions on the basis of their intuition and general observation, they now try to reach more precise and meaningful answers through the use of questionnaire surveys which compare responses from different social groups.

Surveys in Latin America reveal great differences in the ways that individual citizens and groups think about their government. Some people, who are often called "parochials," remain unaware of government in any sense whatsoever. In a survey of Indian groups around Mexico City in 1922, for example, interviewers found that the Indians were unaware not only of the names of their elected officials but even of the political subdivisions which the officials represented.[1] Latin Americans in isolated, rural areas continue to make up the bulk of the "parochial" category, although the spread of communications media and government programs in rural education and agrarian reform have steadily reduced the proportion of persons who have no conception of their government. As citizens become more aware of government, they often do so initially as "subjects," seeing what government can do to them or for them. Latin Americans recognize that a government can tax them, or build a school for them, or conscript them into the army. Then, as "participants" in their political system, they come to appreciate the range of ways in which they themselves can influence what the government decides to do. Besides voting, they see that they can affect government actions through political parties, through labor unions or the Church, and even through the threat of violence.

As citizens begin to feel that they have some influence on government decisions, an increase occurs in what is called their sense of "political efficacy"—their sense of personal influence and power. Sample surveys pose such questions as "How important are the political opinions and activities of persons like yourself?" From these surveys, political scientists can contrast the responses of different groups and of citizens from different countries. Table 1 indicates the degree of influence that people felt they had on government at the national level and at the local level, where N refers to the number of citizens responding in each group and the percentages refer to the proportion of

[1]Manuel Gamio, *La población del valle de Teotihuacán*, 3 vols. (México: Dirección de Talleres Gráficos, Dependiente de la Secretaría de Educación Pública, 1922), Tomo 2, pp. 263–269.

TABLE 1.  POLITICAL EFFICACY IN DIFFERENT
COUNTRIES AND AMONG DIFFERENT GROUPS[2]

| COUNTRY OR GROUP | NATIONAL EFFICACY (%) | LOCAL EFFICACY (%) | N |
|---|---|---|---|
| United States (national sample) | 75 | 77 | (970) |
| United Kingdom (national) | 62 | 78 | (963) |
| Germany (national) | 38 | 62 | (955) |
| Italy (national) | 28 | 51 | (995) |
| Mexico (urban) | 38 | 52 | (1,007) |
| Turkey (peasants) | 26 | 67 | (6,433) |
| Venezuela (high-level government officials) | 78 | 83 | (99) |
| Venezuela (oil workers) | 34 | 62 | (211) |
| Venezuela (peasants) | 21 | 27 | (183) |

[2]This table is a modification of that which appears in John R. Mathiason, "The Venezuelan Campesino: Perspectives on Change," in Frank Bonilla and José A. Silva Michelena, eds., *A Strategy for Research on Social Policy*, vol. 1 of *The Politics of Change in Venezuela* (Cambridge, Mass.: M.I.T. Press, 1967), p. 139.

those citizens who felt that their opinions and activities *did* influence their government. As one would expect, the level of citizen efficacy is higher in the United States and Britain than it is among Venezuelan peasants or among urban residents in Mexico, but note that, according to the survey data, more high-level government officials in Venezuela felt efficacious than did the members of any other group surveyed. These attitudes in part reflect the degrees of influence that different groups *do* possess. The positions of Venezuelan officials within the governmental structure itself allow more direct participation in government decisions than is had by the Venezuelan peasants who live far from the centers of government, who have only recently come into contact with programs of agrarian reform, and whose daily tasks involve farming rather than politics. Such surveys measure perceptions and attitudes rather than influence itself, however, so that we need to ask how accurately the power which groups *think* they have corresponds with the degrees and types of influence which they actually possess.

## GROUPS AND POLITICAL POWER

Besides looking at the attitudes of citizens and at their direct relationships to government, political scientists study the polit-

Anti-communist poster in Buenos Aires. It says: "Let the children come unto me . . . and . . . (I will give them a gun and teach them to hate their fellow man.) Communism. Don't let this happen!" 1968. (*Samuel L. Baily*)

ical roles and activities of such groups as the Church, the military, labor unions, and students. They look not only at what members of the groups think but also at the actual power which the groups possess and at the various strategies for using that power. They may survey the background and values of group members, analyze the responses of a group to a series of contrasting challenges, or compare patterns of group interaction in one country or in a series of countries or regions. After studying the role of the military in non-Western countries, for example, political scientists have noted that it has proved easier to construct modern, westernized armies than it has to produce effective political parties or efficient civilian bureaucracies.[3] This fact, combined with the coercive power which the military naturally possesses, has meant that military leaders have come to direct many of the new nation-states in Asia and Africa, just as through recent coups they have come again to direct many countries in Latin America. Far more than the military officers of Asia or Africa, those of Latin America have received training in the United States, and the United States government has generally maintained its programs of economic aid after coups by Latin American officers have overthrown elected civilian leaders.

The importance of the military in Latin American politics points up the need to analyze the roles of military men as national leaders. It is often argued that military officers in a developing country must become modern technocrats in order to prepare for modern forms of warfare, and that they acquire national loyalty and desires for industrial development which especially fit them for national leadership. The proportion of technocrats to regular line officers in Latin American armies can easily be exaggerated, however, and the experience of many military men as chief executives indicates that they enjoy no unique ability to spur economic development or to force other groups to work loyally behind developmental programs. Military leaders enforce stability, but stability by itself does not produce a more prosperous society, or an end to poverty among marginal groups, or higher levels of satisfaction and efficacy among most citizens.

[3]Lucien W. Pye, "Armies in the Process of Political Modernization," in Jason L. Finkle and Richard W. Gable, eds., *Political Development and Social Change* (New York: John Wiley & Sons, 1966), p. 380.

Anti–United States graffitti on the walls of the University of São Paolo. It attacks a rightwing organization whose initials are CCC, and associates this organization with the United States by making the CCC spell CoCa Cola. 1968. (*Samuel L. Baily*)

Students, as another important group in Latin American politics, strongly favor change rather than stability. In protesting for social change, students sometimes provoke massive retaliations from police and from military forces, as Mexican students did before and after the 1968 Olympics in Mexico City. Despite suppressions of their activities, however, students have continued in many countries to act directly in politics, in part because higher education has always given them a situation of distinct privilege in Latin America. In the 1970's, with a population well over 200,000,000, this region has graduated only about 100 sanitary engineers and 200 dentists each year. Almost half of the population over the age of fifteen remain illiterate, and, whereas more than half the students in the United States go on for more formal education after high school, only one student in ten does so in Latin America.[4] The limited num-

[4]Tad Szulc, *The Winds of Revolution: Latin America Today—And Tomorrow*, rev. ed. (New York: Frederick A. Praeger, 1965), pp. 63–66.

ber of university graduates and their general upper and upper middle class backgrounds have increased the privileged position of Latin American students. Their general prestige and their traditional ability to escape from police by retreating into the respected sanctuary of university grounds have led student groups to become outspoken advocates of reform. Idealism and the fact that the students have not yet taken regular jobs and become caught up in earning a living also lead them to champion reform. Once the students do obtain jobs and actually begin trying to implement goals which they originally put forward in vague and idealistic terms, many of them begin to feel that change can come most effectively through constructive efforts rather than through violence.

Like the members of most groups which have acquired an actual stake in the social system, laborers and businessmen in Latin America usually work and define situations in terms of their own interests. Most labor unions have been more concerned to raise wages and to improve living conditions for their members than they have been to effect broad change for society

Students putting up Peronist election posters in Buenos Aires. 1973. (*Samuel L. Baily*)

Peronist election poster attacking the brutality and starvation due to unemployment during the former military regime. 1973. (*Samuel L. Bailey*)

as a whole, and some activists criticize them for this orientation.
Excessive wage payments can slow down or reverse general
gains in economic development and prosperity, if they sub-
sidize featherbedding and inefficiency, or divert funds from
investment in new equipment, or prevent gains from technological innovation. Fair wages give laborers a purchasing power
which enables them to buy more goods, thus creating a demand
which provides jobs and income. Excessive wage increases,
however—like those by which Juan Perón gained the support of
Argentine unions after 1946—hurt the economic growth on
which laborers' welfare depends in the long run. Mexican workers, who have accepted moderate wage increases, have benefited in the long run through this policy of restraint.

More generally than their counterparts in Central and South

America, Mexican businessmen have also shown wide social concern, especially in the implementation of the goals of the Mexican Revolution of 1910. Businessmen throughout Latin America affect the process of change through their decisions on wages and investment. They help to determine what areas of industry and agriculture will be expanded and, in particular situations, they may choose to oppose all foreign investments from the United States or Europe, or to send their own investment funds to these foreign areas where they feel that the funds will be safe from taxes or expropriation. Political scientists who study Latin American businessmen find that their patterns of activity depend upon the particular political system in which they live. In Chile, a country which had a strong and influential congress like that of the United States, business associations further their interests by working informally with individual congressmen, just as North American business associations do in the United States. In other countries, where legislatures have very little real power, businessmen work through elected presidents or military leaders whose power is manifest and effective.

With both evident and subtle forms of influence, the Catholic Church has played a more direct role in the politics of Latin America than any religious group has done in the United States. Here in America, where religious pluralism prevails, it is customary for representatives of the Protestant, Catholic, and Jewish faiths to give religious invocations at the conventions of both the Republican and Democratic parties. In Latin America, where censuses list over 90 percent of the population as being Roman Catholic, a Catholic prelate gives the invocations at official state dinners. Latin Americans have now severed most formal, institutional ties between Church and State, but the Church continues to mold ideas and values for many citizens. Less than 20 percent of the population in Latin America attends mass at least once a week, and on any particular issue a person or a family may decide that their own interests differ from those which Church teachings suggest. The influence of Catholic schools and teachings is pervasive, however, especially when it reinforces cultural norms like those which oppose birth control and family planning. Serious splits have developed within the Church as to what its specific social policies should be, but if it were not for these splits, the influence of the Church would continue to be even greater than it is.

## VIOLENCE AND POLITICAL CHANGE

A major concern of both political scientists and political activists is whether violence is necessary or justified to bring about social changes which they believe to be worthwhile. It is utopian to believe that violence, in and by itself, can remake society or end selfishness and exploitation. Those who advocate violence need to have specific, feasible plans for social innovation to institute once violence has opened up the social system to wider possibilities. Even when they do possess such plans, the advocates of restrained violence sometimes find—as did the moderates in the French Revolution of 1789—that unleashed violence tends to feed upon itself and to expand until it turns upon the moderates and makes their plans impossible. Nevertheless, a degree of violence is sometimes necessary in order to reorient power relationships. In the United States, the Revolutionary War won independence from Britain, and the Civil War ended legal slavery in the South. In Latin America, where violence may also be necessary to achieve certain ends, numerous groups resort to it in order to promote their own interests or what they believe to be society's interests.

The group resorting to violence most often has been army personnel. Many military officers in Latin America do not believe in the North American tradition of civilian control over the military, and, since they train professionally in the uses of violence, they are repeatedly in a position to overthrow civilian authorities. Theories of social mobility, guardianship, and the protection of military prerogatives are among the most commonly advanced explanations for the resulting military takeovers or coups. The barracks revolt is one of the traditional avenues to power, prestige, and wealth for Latin American officers, many of whom have found that they could rise most easily in this way from comparatively obscure backgrounds to positions of national prominence. Inheriting the prestige of the Spanish conquistadors and the nineteenth-century liberators, officers in Spanish-American countries have seen themselves as guardians of the political order with the right to take over the government when the situation seemed to require it. In Brazil also, where the right of military guardianship has been written into constitutions, the miliary once again came to rule in 1964 in response to skyrocketing inflation, economic mismanagement, and a leftward drift in politics under President João Goulart. Since 1930, the Argentine military has repeatedly intervened. With the 1966 take-over of General Juan Carlos Onganía, military men talked of remaining in power for at least ten years, but finally turned the government over to civilians in 1973.

Although the recent military governments of Brazil and Argentina have refrained from massive enrichment of the military leaders themselves, protection of the basic prerogatives of the military has helped to motivate these and other interventions. When an American political scientist went to study a military take-over in Ecuador in 1963, for example, he at first hypothesized that, in overthrowing a government which did not appear to be acting decisively enough against the Communists, military men had intervened because of their class-based rejection of Communist programs, because of their religious objections to Communism, or because of a feeling that their duty was to maintain order against the threat of Communist violence. When he interviewed the leaders of the take-over, however, he found that their action had little to do with their class, their religion, or their sense of order. They had acted more from the standpoint of professional self-interest than from any other motive, because they had feared that a Communist victory would have replaced the professional army with a civilian militia.[5] Similar concern for the positions of individual officers or the military group as a whole seems to have operated also in the 1968 military coup in Panama, where an important officer felt threatened by President Arnulfo Arias, and in the 1968 take-over in Peru, where the military felt threatened by the Aprista Party, its traditional enemy, in an upcoming election. Although the causes for any coup are multiple rather than sin-

[5]Martin C. Needler, *Anatomy of a Coup d'Etat: Ecuador, 1963* (Washington, D.C.: Institute for the Comparative Study of Political Systems, 1965), pp. 40–41.

gular, the self-interest of those involved operates here as it does in so many power confrontations.

Self-interested involvement in violence also characterizes other Latin American groups. Students and Catholic leaders have figured prominently in many coups; they have fought for university autonomy and the rights of the Church as well as to oppose dictatorial governments. Even where they do not undertake violence, students and church leaders play more active and direct roles in Latin American politics than they do in the United States. In sharp contrast to the apparent self-satisfaction of many labor union members in the United States at the present time, Latin American labor unions sometimes threaten violence in support of their demands. In a book based upon interviews and research carried on while he was still a student in college, a young political scientist has pointed out that the threat of violence can be labor's most effective weapon. Under the free government of Manuel Prado in Peru between 1956 and 1962, the best way for labor to achieve its demands was through threats to the position of the president himself; this is because the president felt vulnerable to overthrow and because labor's votes and economic pressure had less weight than they do in the United States.[6] Except for Mexico which has remained free from violent coups since the 1930's, violent changes in governments have resulted from the pressing of interest group demands in the great majority of Latin American countries.

Since such coups and narrow "revolutions" have served largely as a barrier to social innovation, some Latin Americans assume that a new type of revolution will be necessary in order to orient the process of modernization along more constructive lines. The term "revolution" often connotes major alterations in social structure and in the power relationships among different classes and social groups, but most "revolutions" in Latin America have brought no such alteration. Instead, as coups rather than fundamental revolutions, they have merely changed the personnel of government, leaving intact the prevailing patterns

[6]See "Worker Organizations and the Executive," chapter 3 in James L. Payne, *Labor and Politics in Peru: The System of Political Bargaining* (New Haven, Conn.: Yale University Press, 1965).

of landholding, social structure, and political power. The coups have often allowed individuals to rise from poverty to power, as they did in the cases of Rafael Trujillo or Fulgencio Batista. Trujillo governed the Dominican Republic from his take-over in 1930 until his murder in 1961, while Batista led successful coups in Cuba in 1933 and 1952, only to be overthrown by the forces of Fidel Castro in 1958. Where such men as Trujillo or Batista have gained power, they have often become content with their own position and not tried to reorient their societies in order to make new opportunities available for the majority of citizens. In nationalizing industry, rejecting traditional dependence upon the United States, and trying fundamentally to reorient patterns of social mobility and social structure, the "revolution" which Fidel Castro has pursued since 1959 refers to a process of change far more basic than the struggles by which Trujillo, Batista, or even Castro himself came to power.

The effects of a revolution depend more upon the individual leaders whom it puts into office, and upon the specific programs which they try to implement, than upon the degree of violence which the revolution entails. Violence itself does not bring effective change and reform. In Colombia, for example, about 100,000 persons died in the War of a Thousand Days at the turn of the century, and more than 200,000 have died in the *violencia* between the Liberal and Conservative parties since 1946. Despite its impetus to the formation of a United Front system in which the presidency alternates between the Liberals and Conservatives every four years and in which each party is to have equal representation in the legislature between 1958 and 1974, the Colombian *violencia* has failed to induce effective reform programs. Reforms have come much more directly from the insight and leadership of such men as Carlos Lleras Restrepo, the economist who became president of Colombia in 1966. Some exponents of revolution claim that violence is necessary in order to throw out the "ruling oligarchy," but such a plan would deprive Latin America of many talented leaders. Men from well-to-do families such as Lleras Restrepo or Eduardo Frei of Chile are among the most dedicated reformers in their countries. Such leaders may use the specter of violence in order to induce others to accept peacefully social and economic changes, but, to the extent that it is successful in such policies, violence is not in fact necessary to achieve a social revolution.

## STRATEGIES FOR DEVELOPMENT

The types of "social revolution" which Latin American leaders now call for encompass varying degrees of change in economic relationships, group power and influence, and individual attitudes. Although we often study parts of this process under headings like "economic development" or "political modernization," an economist or political scientist has to reach well beyond his own discipline in trying to understand the process as a whole. Furthermore, in attempts to achieve a more "developed" society where more people can enjoy adequate living standards and greater power to shape their own lives, an almost infinite number of strategies is possible. In analyzing reform strategies that involve combinations of violence, consensus-building, and the reliance for support upon particular groups, political scientists keep in mind the long-run outcome of present policies, the alternative strategies available at a given time, and the individualistic concerns which motivate most persons and groups in a political system.

One strategy for reform would be for Latin American states to "modernize" by becoming more like the United States. In relating the North American experience to the developing countries, a leading political scientist has recently written that the United States should more consciously try "to export not merely American technical know-how, but our political ideology and reasonable facsimiles of our political institutions and practices as well."[7] Our emphasis upon freedom and individual initiative has helped to create a political climate in which many citizens in more authoritarian states would prefer to live, and some people feel that freedom and individual initiative remain the surest ways to promote economic growth in the long run.

By what criteria, however, do North Americans decide

[7]Joseph LaPalombara, "An Overview of Bureaucracy and Political Development," in Joseph LaPalombara, ed., *Bureaucracy and Political Development* (Princeton, N.J.: Princeton University Press, 1963), p. 60.

whether or not they should promote their ideology and their political institutions in Latin America, or when and to what extent they should promote them? At various times, North Americans have favored such promotion because of their desire to export freedom and opportunity, their belief that such activities were in the United States national interest, and their conclusion that the activities were necessary to produce economic development and prosperity in other countries. Parts of these justifications for the promotion of North American institutions may, however, contradict one another. Institutions which meet the welfare needs of a developed society do not necessarily fit well with the harsh needs of the development process—the Uruguayans found this out when the export prices on which their welfare state was built deteriorated. Strategies needed for development sometimes contravene democratic decision-making; people are not likely to vote in favor of the hardships and privations which make possible national savings, investment, and development. Since United States institutions are partly applicable and partly contradictory in the Latin American context, North Americans need to be wary of wholesale exportation of their values and their institutions.

At some points, North and South American traditions coincide. The desire to maximize individual freedom and opportunity has, for example, a long tradition in Latin America just as it does in the United States. Although the rhetoric that one hears on the Fourth of July or at meetings of the Organization of American States often exaggerates the degree to which we have realized these goals for all of our citizens, the goals themselves remain a genuine if tenuous bond among many citizens of the Americas. To emphasize these parts of our ideology is to promote certain parts of the ideological traditions of Latin America as well.

Just because we share some of the same goals, however, does not mean that Latin Americans can achieve these goals in an institutional framework which copies our own. Their constitutions have frequently followed ours in an attempt to reach similar objectives, but the constitutions have failed to do so because the Latin American framework of political expectations and relationships has been so different from that of the United States. In the early twentieth century, political scientists believed that the study of constitutions was at the heart of their discipline and that political reform could best be achieved by "constitutional engineering" designed to alter the constitutional framework of government. Latin American experience has indicated that constitutional alterations are not enough; constitutional engineering based upon the United States model has made comparatively little change in the Latin American context of executive predominance, military guardianship, or political loyalties rooted in the personal ties between a leader and his followers.

A survey taken in Cuba in the summer of 1962 indicated that Cuban workers did not place a high value on the traditional forms of North American democracy. After personally interviewing 202 workers in Cuban plants and industries some three and a half years after Fidel Castro came to power, a political sociologist and his wife found that the great majority of workers did not feel that elections should be held soon. The workers' responses to a question on elections appear in Table 2. When Castro was building support for his guerrilla revolution in the 1950's, he had promised to hold free elections and to reinstitute the Constitution of 1940 once his movement gained power. In what some writers have seen as a betrayal of his revolution.[8] Castro later rejected these promises and decided to remain in

TABLE 2.   ATTITUDES OF CUBAN WORKERS
TOWARD ELECTIONS IN 1962[9]

| *Question: Do you believe that the country ought to have elections soon?* | |
| --- | --- |
| ANSWER | N = 202 |
| *No* | 136 |
| *Yes* | 44 |
| *No opinion* | 22 |

[8]Theodore Draper has become one of the most persuasive exponents of the viewpoint of the "revolution betrayed." See Theodore Draper, *Castro's Revolution: Myths and Realities* (New York: Frederick A. Praeger, 1962); and Thodore Draper, *Castroism: Theory and Practice* (New York: Frederick A. Praeger, 1965).

[9]Maurice Zeitlin, *Revolutionary Politics and the Cuban Working Class* (Princeton, N.J.: Princeton University Press, 1967), p. 38.

personal command of Cuban politics in order to institute the harsh, potentially unpopular reforms which he felt were needed in order to reach the social and economic goals which he had also promised. Democratic elections did not have any substantive meaning for Cuban workers, any more than they do for most Brazilian or Argentine workers, because the elections had not provided a meaningful choice which actually influenced the workers' lives.

The rejection of electoral democracy by Cuban workers in 1962 does not show that the same proportion of other Cuban groups would have similarly rejected it, or that the same number of workers would reject it today. Many upper middle class and upper class Cubans who had especially benefited from the kind of "democracy" which elections had actually brought to Cuba became alienated from Castro over the rejection of his promises, and a large segment of these classes went into voluntary exile. The anti-election attitudes of Cuban workers probably reflect their personal loyalty to Castro, their fear after the Bay of Pigs invasion in 1961 that elections might bring in a weaker government, and their satisfaction with the ways in which the Castro revolution had affected their personal interests through greater job opportunities. Also, Castro's cry of "Why have elections?" had a true ring for many Cubans because their own experience had taught them that "free elections" in Cuba meant something very different from what they have meant in the United States.

Despite past failures in the transplantation of constitutional frameworks and in the implementation of genuinely free elections, selective borrowing and adaptation of some foreign institutions might help Latin Americans to achieve their goals. Large, integrated, and long-lasting political parties have helped to regulate conflict and provide for peaceful change in such countries as Britain and the United States. In Latin America, on the other hand, parties have often been so small and so numerous as to make electoral choices among them unclear, so short-lived as to collapse after an electoral defeat, and so attuned to the interests of a single leader or a narrow group that they could not have brought broad-based reform even if they had come into power. The recent, contrasting experiences of the Revolutionary Party in Mexico, and Acción Democrática in Venezuela indicate the positive role which strong, reform-oriented parties can have in Latin American countries. Although most North Americans are proud of the traditional operation of our two-party system, single-party and multi-party systems like those of Mexico and Venezuela have brought more reform in Latin America than has the two-party system of Colombia. The Mexican system encourages wide competition *within* the Revolutionary Party, while the new strength of the Christian Democrats in Venezuela shows that reform leadership from one party may be possible even where many parties still actively compete for support.

On the basis of this experience, North Americans should consider at least two things when they decide to "promote" institutions such as stronger political parties. First, our *example* and its effectiveness in solving our own problems will win more support in Latin America than will boasts about North American "democracy." Secondly, in discussing the ways in which one country can benefit from the political experience of another, we should ask what *aspects* of a political process or institution may be transferable rather than simply seeking to transfer the process or the institution as a whole.

As North Americans think of what our relations with Latin America should entail, they frequently discuss our "national interest." This concept suggests that, despite moralistic or humanitarian protestations from government officials or private citizens, our policies will ultimately be determined by the power relationships between the United States and Latin America and by our attempt to maximize the benefits which our own country can derive from them. What is the national interest of the United States in relation to Latin America, however? Should we support new programs of foreign aid, or an expansion of American business overseas, or try to help Latin America by paying more for its exports? When we land marines to oppose Communist influence and protect American citizens as we did in the Dominican Republic in 1965, does the fear and opposition which our intervention generates outweigh the benefits which we are said to gain from "stabilizing" the situation and from once again demonstrating our military power? Are C.I.A.–sponsored overthrows of Latin American governments acceptable when they succeed as in Guatemala in 1954, and do they become unacceptable only when they fail as at the Bay of Pigs in 1961?

One problem in arriving at easy answers to such questions is that the overall national interest of the United States is made up of a series of the diverse, often conflicting interests of different groups, governmental agencies, and specific programs both at home and abroad. Political leaders need to weigh the interests against one another and against their possible results both in Latin America and in the United States. In seeking solutions to this problem, a specialist in Soviet politics has recently written that "we should define our national interests in terms of sufficient breadth and vision that they will have relevance for people in all countries who are our natural allies."[10] Certainly we have always felt that the Latin Americans are our natural allies. If they are to continue to be so, we must arrive at better understanding of the political problems which they face, and seek out areas and policies where the national interests of our different states genuinely coincide. To do so more effectively will require systematic study and coordinated actions in both North and South America.

One way to prepare for more effective actions is to uncover the real patterns of power and influence in contemporary Latin America. In order to establish meaningful strategies for development, Latin Americans need to understand these patterns of influence more precisely. Individuals need to be able to stand outside their personal visions of politics and government, to be able to appreciate the attitudes, goals, and interrelationships of other persons and groups in their society. Such a viewpoint would give them more insight into the complexity of power relationships, illustrating, for example, that violence is not a romantic or utopian end in itself, but only one of a series of ways to work for change. If the United States is to be any more than a sympathetic observer of Latin America, then it is also important for our public officials, businessmen, and citizens to understand better the real nature of Latin American power relationships. Moreover, since political science is a broad rather than a parochial discipline, the study of power and influence in any context adds to the basic store of data and interpretation. By reaching sounder conclusions concerning political processes in Latin America, we can, through contrast and comparison, come to better understand ourselves.

[10]Marshall D. Shulman, *Beyond the Cold War* (New Haven, Conn.: Yale University Press, 1966), p. 109.

# 5. SCIENCE, TECHNOLOGY, AND THE PEOPLE OF LATIN AMERICA

## Maurice Bazin

*Maurice Bazin, Associate Professor of Physics at Rutgers University, has studied and visited Latin America on his own for many years and his concern for the future of the area is deep. He begins his essay by asking: 1. can basic scientific research help Latin America develop; 2. are science and technology of direct relevance to the masses of Latin America; and 3. what is the relationship between Latin American countries and the United States as far as the training and use of scientific personnel is concerned? He concludes that Latin America does not need sophisticated scientific technology or the scientific brain power of the United States to solve its most pressing problems because those are a consequence of political realities and not primarily of the technological level of development. The uses to which technology is put are determined by the existing social order. It is useful to compare these conclusions with those of the essay of Turner (Chapter 4).*

T HE LANDING OF MEN ON THE MOON is often regarded as the best example of the success of modern technology and science. We all are excited by the technical details of the packaging of the dehydrated food taken along by astronauts and we watch the maneuvers of the astronauts directly on the living room television set as they place complicated instruments on the surface of the moon a quarter of a million miles away. Landing on the moon does not directly affect the quality of our lives, but we like to view it as a symbol of the potential of technology and science to serve human needs.

Let us contrast this potential with the life being led by most Latin Americans today. Will the people living in Latin America, for example, a peasant from the northeast of Brazil, be able to share our excitement? Should he feel, as we might be tempted to do, that technology makes his society strong and "successful"? He has to contrast the exciting possibility of eating dried meat in a state of weightlessness in space with the fact that he and his family eat meat only once every few weeks on special festive occasions. Should it matter to him that men can communicate through space when he has had no news from his sister for several years since she left for Copacabana as housemaid for a rich family? As for television, he once watched with awe a flickering screen housed in the pedestal of a late dictator's statue in the central square of a seaside resort village. He himself had recently come to the village barefoot after being thrown off a cocoa plantation by the supervisor who had "rented" him for the harvest.

Will the many Latin Americans who live in Spanish-speaking ghettos in the heart of our own cities draw more satisfaction from the technological civilization around them than a Brazilian peasant could? A young emigrée from the Dominican Republic or Puerto Rico will be taking night courses in keypunching in New York while, a block away, huge computers devise rocket trajectories with refined mathematical accuracy. She has been led to believe that "making it" in our technical society requires training through that keypunching course. So far, she

Zé, a man of northeast
Brazil. (*Mary Belfrage*)

has only exchanged the company of the rats who roam the gutters of her street in the old town of Santo Domingo for those of Lenox Avenue in Harlem, but she views as success the possibility of finding someday a "technical" nine-to-five job punching holes in IBM cards for some company.

The technological world familiar to us in the United States is foreign to most Latin Americans and it can crush them with its mechanical might—although ideally it should make it possible for everyone to live a happier life. Technology must be bent to serve the needs of the great masses of Latin America and to enhance their own culture. Therefore, when we ask any question about science and technology in Latin America, we shall ask what its relevance is to the well-being of the people of Brazil or the Dominican Republic or of Latin America at large. We are not interested in the detailed activities of research institutes where scientists enjoy good salaries and comfortable libraries. What we are concerned with is how their work contributes to or hurts the development of their countries, that is, improves or worsens the welfare of its population both physically and mentally. Similarly, when considering the scientific data available in the form of various statistics about Latin America, we shall insist upon connecting the use of these numbers with human life and values, with the pains and joys of human beings.

As a scientist looking at the situation in Latin America, I shall ask certain questions:

1. Can basic scientific research help Latin America now?

2. What kind of scientific activities will aid the development of Latin American societies?

3. What is the relationship between Latin America and the United States regarding scientific and technical personnel?

4. What do we learn when we look "scientifically" at the data concerning the welfare of Latin Americans?

As we answer these questions we shall come to realize that scientific advances and technological methods have not benefited the majority of Latin Americans. It will become clear that science is most often used by upper class elites to foster their own advancement only, and that technology has not yet served the interests of the population at large.

## SOME ATTEMPTS AT USING SCIENCE AND TECHNOLOGY TO FOSTER DEVELOPMENT IN LATIN AMERICA

Several physicists,* eminent in their specialized fields (usually theoretical elementary particle physics), have advocated the creation of fundamental research centers in Latin America as a remedy for underdevelopment. They envision that such centers will play a seeding role in fostering rational decision-making in the country. Probably influenced by their own privileged role in this country as government advisers in politico-military matters, these physicists advocate that the prime minister of

*We shall systematically avoid the use of specific references within the text of this essay. Suggested reading material and original sources are given in the References at the end of the essay.

each underdeveloped country create a secretariat for science and then establish centers for research in basic science. The hope is that such centers will influence the development of applied research which will in turn be useful to the country at large. A further aim of such proposals is to form an intellectual elite of scientists whose wisdom might eventually seep through into the whole society. To put such a proposal into effect one physicist recommended sending 200 scientists from the United States every year into fifty countries. What he totally overlooked is that this figure represents less than one-tenth of the scientists who go in the other direction every year, that is, scientists from underdeveloped countries who emigrate to the United States. Thus the solution proposed is totally out of proportion with the problem at hand and represents the rather typical uninformed idealistic viewpoint of people disconnected from the realities of the third world.

Other concrete examples prove that such approaches have met with failure in Latin America for specific reasons. In Argentina a military government which took over in 1966 harassed university personnel, sometimes requiring oaths of allegiance. Nearly all of the physics staff at the University of Buenos Aires left Argentina. Students from this university, presently residing in the United States, point out that even without the attitude of the military, the Faculty of Sciences was in fact producing research physicists whose only career opportunity was emigration. The reason is that most industrial companies established in Argentina are controlled from the United States and that all the basic research in their fields is performed within the United States.

In the northeast of Brazil a research center was planned for the pursuit of graduate studies. But there was no staff to teach advanced courses and the center then reverted, quite correctly and fruitfully, to attempting to improve and coordinate the teaching of science in secondary schools.

In Venezuela, the National Institute of Scientific Research spends a million dollars per year on a nuclear reactor without producing anything new or valuable in physics. Situated high in the hills above Caracas where the climate is bearable, it merely serves to isolate the scientific researchers from the reality of the sufferings of the people in the slums of the sweltering

Caracas, Venezuela. Hillside shanties rise behind the sign which bans any construction on the site: it is a National Park. (*Mary Belfrage*)

city. The reason for the creation of this institute in the first place had been the political need for showcases of the former dictator Pérez Jiménez.

In Uruguay the study of astronomy could constitute a valid scientific endeavor because very few observatories are located in the Southern Hemisphere. But at a time when exciting discoveries are being made every month in the field of radioastronomy, one learns of the closing down of the only radio telescope in Uruguay due to the sudden unexplained withdrawal of financial support by the government. The telescope was originally a gift from the Carnegie Institution of Washington, but continued financial support was not provided for. Thus have local and international political realities again brought total havoc in what might appear a situation of great potential.

Furthermore, the attempts at forming minority elites of scientists have had no influence on the condition of a country short of reinforcing the smug superior attitudes of the affluent ruling circles to which scientists bring the glory of their trade. The notion of developing science has provided administrators with easy means of accumulating titles and acquiring positions on official commissions which have no other tangible output than bureaucratic expansion. While representatives of countries of the Organization of American States meet in the best hotels in Washington, D. C., or Valparaiso, Chile, as an InterAmerican Nuclear Energy Commission, two out of the four nuclear reactors in Brazil are described in the *International Science News* of the U. S. Department of State with the following diplomatic understatement: "Neither of these instruments appear to have been used extensively to date." And while this Commission in its Final Report recommends renewed support of the magazine *Ciencia Interamericana,* published by the Organization of American States, the same magazine goes from a bimonthly to a biannual publication schedule and amounts to some twenty pages which mainly announce paper resolutions and the creation of more commissions. From its pages comes the best example of the politician's misuse of science: the creation of a National Council of Science and Technology in Argentina whose permanent members are simply the president of the country and the ministers of the government themselves!

Whereas there is little question about the justification for basic research in a wealthy, technologically developed country like the United States, it is clear that scientists in Latin America could devote their talents to efforts of more direct relevance to their fellow men. As stated by Lord Bowden, the Minister of State for Education and Science in the British government, little is to be gained from using science as a status symbol: "If a scientist [in a developing country] studied problems of importance to his own community, such as plant life, structure of the soil, . . . properties of fruits and local herbs, he would be able to help his countrymen and realize his full potential as a scientist. . . . I see little return for a developing country having white-coated workers in nuclear laboratories, when the local drains need attention."

Given the conditions which prevail in most Latin American countries, engaging in pure research in specialized centers only takes talent away from immediate human needs. How could one justify the creation of a chemistry center in a country like the Dominican Republic where 25 percent of the women in the island suffer from goiter due to lack of iodine in their daily food and 65 percent of the population is deficient in vitamin C? Organizational talent, knowledge, and personal commitment are immediately needed to attempt to modify the eating habits of the Dominican peasants, who form 70 percent of the population. They must be taught to make use of the iodine-rich products of the sea and consume the vitamin-rich tropical fruits which grow abundantly on the island. The study of complicated molecules can wait for the day when the children of these peasants will have better than today's 20 percent chance of ever finishing elementary school.

Confronted with such political realities and their consequences, the proposals to create nuclei of fundamental scientific research in underdeveloped countries appear rather futile. Furthermore, one should not hesitate to consider them an example of the arrogance of the advisory role taken on by many scientists whose contact with Latin America typically amounts to delivering a few esoteric lectures in English between sunbaths during a few weeks' all-expenses-paid stay in a Latin American university. As the famous British novelist C. P. Snow said pointedly at the University of Missouri in November 1968, "It is contemptuous to tell people who will starve that 'man does not live by bread alone.' "

## THE BRAIN DRAIN

Behind the illusion of creating an indigenous scientific elite in Latin American countries lies not only the lack of local qualified personnel, but more fundamentally, the actual depletion of talent due to emigration to the very same United States. This situation, referred to as the "brain drain," is of such proportions that it has been studied by a special committee of the Congress of the United States. Senator Walter Mondale of Minnesota, talking about the drain of medical doctors from less developed countries, called the situation a "national disgrace": "That we should need doctors from countries where thousands die daily of disease to relieve our shortage of medical manpower is inexcusable." The yearly contribution of the developing countries to U.S. medical manpower is equivalent in numbers to the entire output of the fifteen U.S. medical schools graduating the largest number of M.D.'s. Furthermore, this imbalance is getting greater every day, having gone from a situation in 1951 when only 9 percent of our hospital residents were foreign to 24 percent in 1964 and to more than 30 percent in 1968.

A typical example of the medical situation in Latin America is given by Colombia (for which numbers happen to be available) where there is one doctor per 2,000 persons compared to one doctor per 770 persons in the U.S. Specific examples from Latin America indicate that in a country like the Dominican Republic out of 200 newly graduated physicians in 1962, 78 went to the United States. Maybe every Dominican doctor residing in the United States should be reminded that half of the Dominican children die before reaching the age of five. The overall situation varies greatly from country to country and within each country the cities are always much better provided with doctors than the countryside. The Latin American countries which have an adequate supply of doctors (like Argentina, whose situation is comparable to the United States) do not see their graduates emigrate to other needy Spanish-speaking countries but instead to the United States.

This brain drain exists not only in the field of medicine but also in other professional areas. Argentine engineers who have left for the U.S. in the last decade amount to 8 percent of those graduating in the previous ten years. This exodus from the whole of Latin America especially affects the fields which benevolent advisers suggest to develop most: for instance, among foreign nuclear engineering students in the United States half of those who obtain a master's degree and 73 percent of those who obtain a Ph.D. degree remain in the United States. One should, in fact, question the value of Latin Americans studying nuclear engineering since it is known from United Nations surveys that Latin America is extremely rich in potential hydroelectric resources which are cheaper to use than nuclear reactors for producing electrical energy. Thus the lure of "nuclear" science takes technically competent individuals away from the projects which are best adapted to their countries' potentials and needs.

The most frightening aspect of scientific brain drain from developing countries is its growth over the last ten years: the emigration of physicians rose three-fold, the emigration of engineers rose six-fold, and the emigration of research scientists rose nearly ten-fold. The consequences of such changes can only be grim for the underdeveloped countries.

It is worthwhile to push this numerical analysis a little further and note that the countries which incur the largest losses of scientific personnel are those which receive the largest amount of U.S. aid via the Agency for International Development (AID) in the form of U.S. technicians and financing of university trainees within the foreign country. The overall balance between the brain drain and the aid is a deficit for the underdeveloped country! In the words of the Report to Congress of the Committee on Government Operations: "Thus, in 1967 the United States spent roughly $75 million toward providing some 5,400 trained persons to the very countries engaged in 'exporting' nearly 5,200 of their scientific professionals. The statistical near balance between AID–financed manpower and 'brain drain' outflow is possible only by including U.S. technicians sent to this group of countries. If AID efforts to increase *local* manpower (3,900 AID trainees) is compared to the outflow of local manpower (5,200), AID comes out the loser by 1,300 professionals."

It is true that the emigration from Latin American countries is in part a consequence of the lack of opportunities, frequent corruption in government circles, and political repressions. But by its very aid, the U.S. government maintains in power those reactionary and/or corrupt, and/or military governments from which the educated elites flee. The very wording of the title of the Congressional Report, "Scientific Brain Drain from the Developing Countries" seems to describe a deliberate exploitation of underdeveloped countries by the United States.

Indeed, while this report of 1968 recommends changing immigration laws in order to force foreign scientific personnel from underdeveloped countries to return home after completing their studies in the United States, no change has been put into effect so far by the Department of Immigration. In fact, the immigration laws were modified in 1965 to *facilitate* the immigration of specially qualified technical persons and presented by Secretary of State Dean Rusk with the words, "Our country has the rare chance to be able to attract immigrants of great intelligence and capacity. Immigration, well administered, can be one of our great national resources." As Dr. Parkins, an adviser to President Johnson, put it then, "The immigration policy of the United States has changed. We are no more putting out the call 'give me your tired, your poor, your huddled masses.' Now we say 'give me your most brilliant citizens, the most educated, the most talented, our machines will do the manual work.' "

Today's brain drain can be seen in historical perspective as a continuation of the cultural exploitation of colonial days. One may recall, for instance, that Cuban universities at the end of the last century could not grant any doctoral degrees because the government of Spain, which controlled the island, abolished their right to do so. Thus, any advanced student had to be able to afford going to Spain to obtain a higher education. Today, many universities in the United States and Western Europe take full advantage of the brain drain. Thus, for example, all the full professors on the physics faculty of Rockefeller University in New York come from abroad, and two out of three from underdeveloped countries. These statistics take on added meaning when one remembers the extensive economic interests of the Rockefeller family in Latin America.

## POLITICAL COMMITMENT AND THE USE OF SCIENCE AND TECHNOLOGY

The solutions to specific medical or technical problems in Latin America rarely require any large scale development of scientific studies. They are usually immediately evident once a political commitment to solve them has been made by the country and once its population is made aware of the specifics of the situation. It was not by establishing a pompous "National Hookworm Research Center" that the Cuban government of Fidel Castro attacked and solved the problem of intestinal parasites. Rather it used the most powerful technological tool at its disposal, namely television, and the most powerful human tool, the individual's capacity to understand simple words about worms making holes in the soles of bare feet. Of course, speeches alone would not do if the peasant to whom one were talking could not buy shoes. So a whole economic situation, its priorities, its scale of values, had to be reconsidered.

Let us give one more example of a Cuban solution to a problem. International Conferences of hundreds of technical experts have been held throughout the world without effecting significant results in dealing with the problem of illiteracy. Statistics have been collected for years by international agencies and ministries of education in all Latin American countries. Here is the present situation with respect to "alphabetization," as Latin Americans call the problem, in a few dry scientific percentages (see table on page 88).

The numbers presented here should be taken as optimistic since they almost always come ultimately from local officials who want to make the situation look rosier than it is. Some countries have quite interesting illiteracy rates: Haiti with more than 90 percent at all ages and the U.S.–administered Panama Canal Zone with a rate comparable to the U.S. rate, whereas the country of Panama itself which surrounds it has a "usual" 30 percent illiteracy rate. (How come there is apparently no influence by the Canal Zone upon Panama's education?) The only independent country which has nearly eradicated illiteracy is Cuba. (It had an official 25 percent illiteracy rate before the revolution.) Again, Cuba did this not via scientific institutes but by the involvement of a whole enthusiastic population, a very simple solution which consisted of sending into the interior of the country for nine months 100,000 young people who had graduated from secondary school. The only weapons which they carried were pencils, notebooks, and a kerosene lamp. They were called the "literacy brigades Conrado Benitez" in memory of one of them who many believe was assassinated by agents of the U.S. Central

## PERCENTAGE OF ILLITERATE BY AGE GROUP AND COUNTRY (1960)

| AGE | COLOMBIA | DOMINICAN REPUBLIC | GUADELOUPE MARTINIQUE | GUATEMALA | VENEZUELA | CUBA* |
|---|---|---|---|---|---|---|
| 10–20 years | 15 | 23 | 7 | 56 | 23 | 15,~0 |
| 21–34 years | 22 | 25 | 14 | 59 | 27 | 20,~0 |
| 35–65 years | 34 | 50 | 30 | 65 | 46 | 30, 5 |

*Estimates for 1950 and 1965.

Intelligence Agency. They put in practice the words of José Martí, *"ser culto para ser libre"* (to be educated in order to be free).

This was a political solution involving a significant fraction of the population; it did not come from the drop by drop dispensing of superior knowledge by a scientific elite. It involved the people at large, their informed consent, and their enthusiasm. It would have had no value if it had been a one-shot affair. But it was continued and built upon by many other basically political decisions: the building of schools, the creation of self-improvement night courses for workers. It was no show; it was real. Meanwhile, instead of following this example, self-declared experts and scholars publish Ph.D. theses devising long-range plans to normalize curricula of the secondary schools of Venezuela or Mexico where 95 percent of the population never reaches that level of schooling.

## THE FORGOTTEN HUMAN STATISTICS

The statistics on illiteracy which we have presented, however illuminating they may be, provide a picture of only one aspect of the situation of the people of Latin America. One might still visualize "happy Indians" eating the abundant fruit from tropical trees in never-ending sunshine in countries "rich in mineral ores of all types." This idealistic view would indeed apply to the tiny segment of the population in which all riches are concentrated (the famous "5 percent who own 95 percent of the land"). For all other Latin Americans, the question of life and death, of sheer subsistence, comes first—every day.

Let us look at some statistics which convey the harsh realities of human suffering. Behind every figure representing large production of minerals or exotic fruit loom the no less impressive figures representing life standards of miners or agricultural workers. Technology has generally been used to raise the production figures without having any effect on the workers' life standards. We shall, therefore, put side by side economic statistics and "human" statistics. (We must point out that the economic type of statistics is the one which most often finds its way into textbooks, or in standard 500-page books like *Indus-*

*trialization of Latin America* [McGraw-Hill], or in the guide book used by British tourists and businessmen, *The South American Handbook* [Trade and Travel Publication Ltd., London]. The other type of statistics is only available from sources which have no vested economic interests in the countries being studied, like the *UNESCO Yearbook* or the reports of journalists.)

This is an industrial skills school set up and maintained by the government in Valdivia, in southern Chile. The programs are designed to train youth in the new skills they need for factory work. (*Batya Weinbaum— courtesy UNICEF*)

Consider the production of tin in Bolivian mines which provide close to 50 percent of all the tin used in the United States (an impressive fact in itself). Fifty million pounds are produced annually with a "value" of fifty million dollars. Without asking the economic question of who pockets this "value," we may simply look at how the miners who extract this ore live. The human statistics reveal that 50 percent is indeed a key figure for tin production in the Bolivian Andes: 50 percent of the children in the town of Colquiri (30,000 inhabitants) die before the age of one; 50 percent of the miners contract tuberculosis; and another 50 percent have syphilis. Their life expectancy of 35 years is roughly 50 percent of the life expectancy in the United States. To put it into monetary terms: they earn one dollar per day of work and this is the "value" of one pound of tin, as quoted by the economists.

In light of these statistics, would the life of the Brazilian peasant or the Bolivian tin miner be changed if one of their countrymen received a Nobel prize for research in basic science or if one of their countrymen went to the moon? The facts are simply that Americans do get the Nobel prizes and do go to the moon while the Food and Agriculture Organization of the United Nations warns that Latin Americans have a growing chance to starve with every passing day.

## CONCLUSION

Although we have examined the Latin American situation in a critical way with regard to the role of science in the lives of its people, we have tacitly assumed that science and technology should play a significant role in the evolution of the under-developed countries. It would be a useful lesson in humility for our scientists to put this very assumption in doubt. Categorizing other countries as "underdeveloped" by measuring their achievements in term of our own technological standards is a rather complacent and self-righteous way of affirming our superiority. We usually assume that underdevelopment exists only in the Third World. Is it not possible that an underdeveloped country may be more developed culturally or have higher human values than our own? Are not the musical intricacies of the sambas from Bahia as sophisticated as the designs of electronic circuits? Certainly they are more directly enjoyable by everyone. We easily assume that developed countries are the only ones which have something to teach, while the role of the third world is simply to learn. It may be we who have to learn again how to listen to other human beings.

## REFERENCES

The main statistical data come from the *United Nations Statistical Yearbook*.
The Brain Drain data come from the House Report No. 1215 of the

Men dancing at the harbor in Bahía, Brazil. (*Maurice Bazin*)

90th Congress; 23rd Report by the Committee on Government Operations, March 28, 1968; William L. Dawson, Chairman. Original sources include unpublished reports by the "Study Project on the Migration of Scientists and Physicians" (1968) of the Adlai Stevenson Institute of International Affairs, Robie House, 5757 South Woodlawn Avenue, Chicago, Ill. 60637.

The conventional attitude of American physicists is best exemplified by M. Moravcsik, *Minerva* 2, 197 (1964).

Other data come in part from M. Niedregang's *Les 20 Amériques Latines,* Plon, Paris, 1962; C. Belfrage's *The Man at the Door with the Gun,* Monthly Review Press, New York, 1963; K. King's "Malnutrition in the Caribbean" in *Natural History,* Jan. 1970, p. 64; Franklin de Oliveira's "A Guerra Civil Oculta" in *Revolucao e Contra—Revolucao No Brazil,* Editora Civilizacao Brasileira, Rio de Janeiro (1962).

# 6. STUDYING LATIN AMERICA

## Ronald T. Hyman

*Ronald T. Hyman, Associate Professor at the Rutgers University Graduate School of Education and author of several books on teaching, looks at Latin America as a curriculum and teaching specialist. He suggests that we approach the study of Latin America by utilizing the key concepts of the various social sciences —many of which have been set forth in previous chapters—in our search for answers to important public issues. He further argues that we must study Latin America through "open inquiry," a method also suggested by Baily and Turner (Chapters 2 and 4), and with this in mind he gives sample questions concerning the topic of militarism.*

IN THE PRECEDING ESSAYS each social scientist has looked at Latin America from the point of view of his own subject. In doing so each has identified several *key concepts* with which to organize the facts he presents. Safa, an anthropologist, uses the concept of subculture to organize her material in "more specific categories within which contemporary Latin American cultures can be compared and grouped." Turner, a political scientist, uses the concepts of power and influence to ask questions about the behavior of governments and their citizens. Baily, a historian, employs the concepts of uniqueness of man and uniqueness of events as well as a broad time perspective in his efforts to understand Latin America. Street, an economist, presents two schools of thoughts (monetarist and structuralist) as he treats the concepts of specialization, inflation, and standard of living.

The importance of key concepts is that they enable us to organize and understand the overwhelming amount of information related to life in Latin America; they establish the common features which give meaning to specific, isolated facts. Many of the social science concepts are used in not one but several fields. Just as economists and sociologists use the concept of power, which is primarily identified with political science, so do political scientists use the concepts of subculture and specialization from sociology and economics. Each field borrows some concepts primarily identified with other fields. There is overlap since all the social sciences have one common focus—man. However, it is the particular grouping of key concepts which sets one social science off from another in spite of obvious similarities among fields.

When we use key concepts, we use what is important in a social science. We focus on what the scholars, men who devote their professional careers to research and teaching in a field of knowledge, consider to be the essence of their field. Thus, with the key concepts of economics we concentrate on what is central to economics rather than on what is trivial.

The problem for most people, however, is to combine the

key concepts of the separate social sciences in order to gain the fullest understanding of Latin America. One way of integrating the social sciences is to focus on a *public issue* when we organize our facts. By "public" we mean that which affects the community at large, in contrast to "private," or that which affects only an individual or a small group of individuals. By "issues" we mean controversy and disagreement about matters which affect the larger community. For example, what to do about air pollution in our cities is a public issue. Public issues arise because there is conflict among people as to what is best for the community. Since people disagree as to what is good and right, they disagree about solutions to community problems. Sometimes public issues arise because the central values we hold—such as individual liberty, justice, human dignity, equal opportunity, majority rule, national security, and personal property—are not specifically defined. Sometimes public issues arise because people disagree about which values are most important. For example, a public issue may arise when a group of engineers backed by the city government (majority rule) proposes tearing down some rows of private homes (per-

This is the classroom of an agricultural skills school in southern Chile. It is the converted mansion of an appropriated estate (*asentamiento*). Ninety students and their teachers live and study here, and work and run the farm. (*Batya Weinbaum—courtesy UNICEF*)

sonal property) for a new superhighway. Should the engineers' proposal be accepted?

To show how this integration of the social sciences can be done let us take an example of a major broad topic of concern within Latin America. Let us take as our example the role of the military in Latin America. We can use this topic to show how the various social sciences offer the key concepts and facts needed to understand the role of the military, which is in turn central in understanding Latin American life. Rephrased in question form, this topic serves as an example of a major public issue facing the U.S. as an influential world power. The public issue is: should the U.S. government officially recognize and/or support (that is, exchange ambassadors, grant loans, give weapons, and so forth) a Latin American government established by military take-over of a previously elected government? In the 1960's there were many such take-overs and perhaps in the 1970's there will be more. What should our country's policy be toward these countries?

Let us take a specific example in its barest form as a starting point to help demonstrate this integrated approach: on April 27, 1969 the constitutionally elected president of Bolivia, Rene Barrientos, died in a helicopter crash. Immediately afterward, Vice-President Luis Adolfo Siles was sworn in as president to serve until the next election scheduled for August, 1970. However, on September 27, 1969, General Alfredo Ovando assumed the presidency of Bolivia in a military take-over from Luis Siles.*

The specific basic question is: should the U.S. government officially recognize and support the government of General Ovando (Torres or Bunzer)?

To arrive at a reasonable decision on this policy question we must first acknowledge that it is made up of several different types of questions with different types of answers.

---

*On October 6, 1970, General Ovando was overthrown by General Juan José Torres who in turn was overthrown less than a year later by General Hugo Bunzer. This does not negate the importance of our example, however, because the public issue of recognizing a foreign government remains the same no matter how many upheavals there are. One might also subject the September 1973 military coup in Chile to the same kind of analysis.

*Questions of Definition.* What do we mean by a *military take-over?* If Siles, the constitutionally legitimate president, agreed to step down in favor of General Ovando, was this a military take-over? If Siles refused to step down and Ovando forcefully removed him, was this a military take-over?

*Questions of Information.* What are the facts surrounding General Ovando's take-over? Was the Barrientos-Siles government corrupt or dictatorial? What groups of Bolivians supported Siles? What groups supported Ovando? Why did General Ovando take over the government rather than run for election? (The *New Republic* magazine of October 18, 1969 states that Ovando represented the rural poor and that "they are impatient with citified ways, with books and ballots, with courts and constitutions. They understand action. If Barrientos is dead and Ovando is to succeed him, let him do it." Is this position by the *New Republic* acceptable?)

*Questions of Values.* Was it right for General Ovando to overthrow the constitutional government of Siles? If it was not right, should our government recognize General Ovando as the president of Bolivia? Should the U.S. support General Ovando's government in light of the fact that it took over the Bolivian Gulf Oil Company, a corporation owned privately by U.S. citizens?

*Looking at the Future.* What will probably happen if we do (or do not) support the government of General Ovando? Will denial of U.S. recognition and financial and military aid lead to a take-over by an anti-U.S. group?

*Looking for Similarity.* Was our revolution in 1776 a military take-over of a legitimate government? Was our military action right? In what ways is our 1776 situation similar (and not similar) to the Bolivian situation of 1969?

In answering such questions we need the ideas and facts yielded by the various social sciences. We need to turn to political science to understand the nature of Ovando's power and whether or not his government is legitimate; to economics to estimate the potential consequences of withholding economic aid to Bolivia; to anthropology to understand why the rural poor support Ovando; and to history to understand the tradition of frequent military take-overs in Bolivia (185 in 144 years). In addition we need to draw on our own beliefs about right and wrong as well as what we know about the Bolivians' beliefs about right and wrong.

No single type of question and no single social science is sufficient to answer our basic policy question about recognition of General Ovando. The purpose of each is rather to contribute the ingredients we need to arrive at a policy decision. Our task is to blend the answers from each type of question and the concepts from each social science into our policy answers which also must take into account the existing U.S. government policy concerning Latin America.

One further point. In working with the answers to our questions we need to keep in mind that not everything we read, see, or hear is true. Some statements may be bold lies, some may be distortions of the truth, and some may be only one part of the total picture. As open investigators we need to keep in mind the nagging question, "Is this true?" whenever we gather information. If not, we might easily come to an unreasonable decision which will not be based on truthful information.

Many people find it helpful to have a guide to refer to as they go about their investigations. In this way they avoid the slips that occur all too often. Let me, therefore, suggest the following:

*Is this information true?* Does the source of this information have a good reputation for stating the truth? What is the particular slant of the information which shows the viewpoint of the source? Does the information adequately support a reasonable explanation of the event? Is there a time and sequence connection between this information and other information which will establish its truth?

*Are the definitions of the terms used acceptable to most people?* To you? Are the definitions clear? Do the definitions of the terms cover specific examples? (For instance, does our definition of a military take-over cover the Bolivian situation of September, 1969?)

*Is your belief on this issue held by many other people?* Why do you hold this belief? If this particular belief conflicts with another important belief, will you give preference to this one? The other one? To a third one more important than both these two? (For example, in regard to your policy toward a Bolivian government, will you support only democratically elected presidents even if they are pro-Russian and anti-U.S.? Or will you support militarily established leaders if they are pro–U.S. and anti-Russian?)

Obviously, there are many other secondary questions that can be posed. But these are enough to get started on open investigation. They will serve as a prod to ask further questions which are a necessary part of our overall investigation of Latin America. By focusing our questions on public issues based on broad topics we have a good way of integrating the key concepts and information of the various social sciences. With care we can arrive at informed and reasonable positions on these issues. We thus have a suitable approach for studying Latin America.

# INDEX